Quick Charge
Your Life
Unshakable Self-Esteem

TOMMY TURNER

Quick Charge Your Life
Unshakable Self-Esteem

Copyright © 2020 by Tommy Turner

ISBNs: 978-1-7349754-3-7 (Paperback)
       978-1-7349754-4-4 (Hardback)
       978-1-7349754-5-1 (eBook)

All rights reserved. No part of this publication may be reproduced, stored in a retrieval system, or transmitted in any form or by any means—for example, electronic, photocopy, and recording—without the prior written permission of the publisher. The only exception is brief quotations in printed reviews.

Acknowledgment

Each time I sit down to write, I think of just how much I love and appreciate my two children, Kristina and Andrew. I am so fortunate to have them in my life. I will forever acknowledge the love and adoration I have for my children and grandchildren in every book I ever write. I trust I am paving a way and creating a legacy for my kids and grandkids to follow one day. I pray that what I write will not only inspire millions around the world, but that I will lead by example, showing the way for my friends and family to live the *Quick-Charge Life* so that they might experience the joy, peace, passion, and happiness that I do...

I am once again forever grateful for all the professionals who have helped me to finetune my message and book designs. Because of their incredible gifts and talents, I am able to publish these books!

Contents

Introduction 1
1. Are We Headed in the Right Direction? 7
2. What Is Self-Esteem Anyway? 17
3. What Are You Missing? 25
4. Abused and Broken. 33
5. Abused and Broken. 41
6. Is It Pride or Healthy Self-Esteem? 51
7. The Beginning Pages of Life 57
8. Learn to Love Yourself. 63
9. Throw Out the Lemonade 73
10. What's Your Story? 81
11. The Chicken or the Egg? 89
12. You Asked for It. 95
13. Looking Back; Moving Forward. 101
14. The Mirror Is Your Friend 105
15. Addictions 113
16. What About Me? 119
17. Conclusion 123

Books 127
Coming Soon 129
Contact 131

Introduction

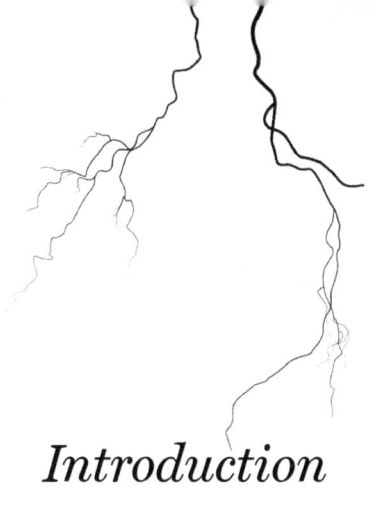

When considering a new topic about which to write for my *Quick Charge Your Life* series, I often choose a topic based on a subject that I have addressed in my own personal life. I love to share my personal insights, failures, weaknesses, and successes along the way in hopes that whoever reads my books will be inspired to break free from whatever holds them back.

I am always collecting new information, watching inspiring videos, reading books, filing notes, writing thoughts, and studying topics that I feel will give me personal strength and knowledge so that I might impart what I learn and thereby inspire others. I am passionate about every topic about which I choose to write in the *Quick Charge* series, and in this case, I hope to offer some inspiration and helpful tools to build an unshakable self-esteem.

If you have not had the opportunity to read my first book in the *Quick Charge* series, which is simply titled *Quick Charge Your Life*, then I would highly encourage you to pick up a copy as it will shed some light on my passion to live life to the fullest. My prayer is that living the quick-charge life will inspire others to move past their perceived limitations and boldly step into the life they were born to create. I *quick charge* every morning, noon, and night!

One of my missions in every book that I write is to embolden individuals to discover their uniqueness, realize their dreams and thrive in this lifetime. However, if you battle with a low self-esteem, believing and/or trusting that living your dreams and thriving in this lifetime is even possible may seem quite difficult for you. Perhaps you don't even know what life you were born to create or how to dream for a brighter future.

One of the purposes of this book is to help those who might struggle with a low self-esteem to take the focus off their own reflection or image for now and instead see God's love shining through His eyes. This book will outline and reveal how to find incredible value and self-worth within yourself. You do have something worth living for and to give back that will inspire others.

I should mention that as I am writing this book, we are in the middle of the Covid-19 world pandemic crisis of 2020. So much is still unknown in our world right now. I see fear in the eyes of people I thought were strong and would never allow anything to shake them. I have family members who have lost their jobs and will never go back to the place they were once gainfully employed prior to the coronavirus outbreak.

I have heard the anxious concerns in the voices of people with whom I cross paths in my business even as I now always observe the social-distancing rules and stay six feet away from them. Watching people interact with one another right now looks so odd to me. I watch people who seem almost afraid even to look at each other for fear of contracting the Covid-19 virus.

Now, please understand, I am in no way making light of this horrific world pandemic crisis. I do know and understand that people have lost loved ones due to this virus. I am certain

Introduction

this pandemic will alter the lives of millions and create new directions and plans for many.

However, I do wonder what future encounters between humans will look like when we are allowed to return to a somewhat normal lifestyle again. How will we start interacting with one another in our social circles?

Will we hesitate to shake the hand of a new acquaintance as a prelude to saying hello? Perhaps we will simply nod the next time rather than shaking the hand of a client in order to seal a business transaction. We are already a society that has become less and less interactive on a personal level. People would rather send a quick text or an email rather than make a phone call. Families sit and stare at their phones all evening rather than interreact and talk to one another. In fact, some choose to send texts back and forth rather than talk to one another while sitting in the same room only ten feet away from each other!

Now, because of the scare of infection from this Covid-19 virus or the next virus or the next…I wonder what will happen. Will world leaders determine to eliminate handshakes, hugs, and kisses on the cheek as normally accepted ways of greeting one another? However, I think what I really want to know is how the lack of touch will affect the self-esteem of the many who already feel insecure about themselves. A future possibility certainly exists that no one will even be willing to make physical contact with others. This possibility is a REAL concern of mine because I believe basic human touch and connection is essential to a person's self-image and wellbeing.

Seeing what life is like one year, two years, or more down the road from right now could be noticeably interesting. Perhaps as you are reading this book, it is already a few years past the

2020 Covid-19 pandemic scare, and many of the questions I have at this very moment will have already been answered.

I do feel very strongly that WE, as a people, a nation, and even as a world will never go back to the so-called "normal" way of living prior to this pandemic. I choose to believe that many will come out better, stronger, thankful, and humbler! I genuinely believe many who might not have found the courage prior to this pandemic will proceed to accomplish great things in life.

Trust me, I do not take this virus lightly. I understand that many have legitimate fears and concerns, especially if their lives were touched directly either physically or financially. However, implementing the techniques and mindset outlined in this book can help build an unshakable self-esteem—even in the midst of a crisis.

As sure as I am that many will come out on top, I can also imagine that many will potentially develop a low self-esteem that is causally related to this world event. Due to circumstances beyond their control, some people who were doing very well prior to the outbreak have now lost every bit of security they have ever known and feel like giving up.

I am experiencing devasting changes in my own personal life causally related to this pandemic, but I am eagerly looking for new opportunities that abound everywhere. I am confident that I will rise above and come out better than before, and I am believing you will too.

Since most people will be reading this book long after the pandemic is over or at least I certainly hope the crisis is over by the time this book is officially published, I trust whether or not you were directly affected by the Covid-19 virus that the following pages will prove to be life-changing. I have written this book in order to offer a new perspective and hope for a

Introduction

brighter future! As you read, you'll discover many valuable tools that can be applied to your life, including how to change your life's view and climb your mountain to rise above your circumstances and build an unshakable self-esteem.

My friend, let's start climbing!

"For I know the plans I have for you," declares the LORD, *"plans to prosper you and not to harm you, plans to give you hope and a future."*
— JEREMIAH 29:11 NEW INTERNATIONAL VERSION (NIV)

Learn it, live it, and inspire others! *Quick Charge Your Life! Unshakable Self-Esteem!*

Adversity, and perseverance and all these things can shape you. They can give you a value and a self-esteem that is priceless."
— SCOTT HAMILTON

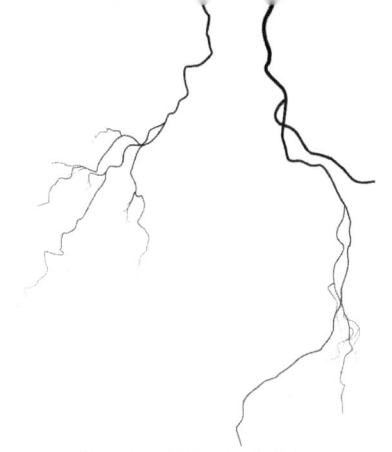

CHAPTER ONE

Are We Headed in the Right Direction?

When I begin gathering information to start the writing process for a new book, one of my first steps is to search for all the books I can find related to the topic about which I am writing. Admittedly, I do not read all of the books or even half the books I discover, but I will often read a few of the more popular books on the topic that I am researching.

I also make certain to examine a few books with closely related or similar topics as well. If I am in a bookstore, I often browse several related books on the bookshelf by checking out the covers, both front and back, the table of contents, and the introduction. On many occasions, I can be found tucked away in the corner of the bookstore settled in a comfy chair reading a chapter or two just to gain some possible insights and ideas for the direction of my book. Barnes & Noble happens to be close to my house and is one of my favorite hideaways.

The next step I take in preparing to write a book is to conduct some preliminary Google searches. As I began my research on this book's topic, I quickly discovered that when searching for the definition and meaning of self-confidence, I found that...ummmm, wait a minute. Are we headed in the right direction? I thought this book was about self-esteem? Well, hold on, my friend, I plan on getting to that subject.

Initially, for my second book, I had chosen to address self-confidence as my main topic of interest. My initial search queries focused on the subject of self-confidence, but when I first started searching for information on self-confidence, the word *self-esteem* more often than not would come up as well. In fact, many times self-esteem came up as the number-one search option—even though I had not even typed the word *self-esteem* anywhere in my search query.

This newfound discovery piqued my interest, and after some additional research and finding that self-esteem continually came up search after search, I wanted to further investigate and break down the differences between *self-confidence* and *self-esteem*. So, I asked Google to compare these two concepts, and the following is the first comparison that came up:

Self-esteem refers to how you feel about **yourself** overall; how much esteem, positive regard or self-love you have. Self-confidence is how you feel about your **abilities** and can vary from situation to situation.

As I continued to examine the two words side-by-side, I discovered that many people who might have a high self-confidence can actually have a low self-esteem. Yes, a person may be very accomplished in a particular ability and have tremendous confidence in his abilities to perform a certain skill. That person, no doubt, possesses a strong self-confidence when he is performing that particular task or skill. Sports athletes, entertainers, artists, business executives are a few examples of people who generally possess self-confidence in their abilities.

Are We Headed in the Right Direction?

However, when these same authorities are sitting at home or possibly even in a room full of people who admire them, they often lack a healthy self-esteem. On the outside, their life would appear to be perfect based on appearance, income, and a myriad of other factors often associated with success. Looking at all the outside factors would suggest they have it all together. However, spectators or onlookers do not have access to what these presumably successful people see and feel about themselves on the inside. We think, *Surely, they must have a healthy self-esteem, right?* Well, perhaps not.

On the other hand, a person might possess a healthy self-esteem, which means they see themselves as worthy and have an overall positive view of themselves, but unfortunately, they may lack self-confidence in the areas they are not good at performing.

I remember watching an online interview featuring Bill Gates and Warren Buffet. Mr. Buffet stated that he chose to give his attention to the one area he could do really well, which of course, was investing. He said he knew how to choose easy companies to invest in, but he also admitted that he had many other shortcomings, failures, and weaknesses. Still, in spite of his weaknesses, he became one of the richest men in the world.

After hearing this interview, my interest in self-esteem became really intrigued. I went to Amazon.com to check out the self-help categories to see what books relating to self-esteem and self-confidence were available. The first glitch I discovered in my research was that the word *self-esteem* was listed in the self-help category, but the word *self-confidence* was NOT found.

As I investigated even further, I felt that if Amazon prioritized *self-esteem* as worthy of being listed as a self-help category and not self-confidence, then perhaps I should take that listing as a nudging to change my main focus to self-esteem. Even as

I would work on a book based on that topic first, I knew that I would likely still flesh out the meaning and significance of self-confidence.

This search then led to other topics I want to explore in the future like self-love, self-image, self-assurance, and many other topics associated with the concept of self-esteem. Who knows, I may still write a *Quick Charge Your Life* book on those topics as my main focus as well one day, but self-esteem seems to be the main direction toward which I am drawn to write for this book in the series.

I often have many thoughts going on inside of my head at one time when I am searching and writing—as you might already be able to tell by my writing style. The creative juices are always flowing, and the thrill of learning, researching, and discovering new information is very satisfying and exciting for me. Every time I find a new path to go down in my learning and discovery, it's truly a *quick-charge* moment for me!

As I was writing and preparing this chapter, I was also thinking, *Do I have a healthy self-esteem?* I then thought about my self-confidence as well. I asked myself, "Self, why do you do the things you do when you begin writing a book? Was this method taught to me? Did I think of it on my own? Is there really a right or wrong way to begin writing a book?"

Hmmm, I thought, *I really do not know the answers to those questions.* But the one thought that did come to my mind during this whirlwind of questions and self-dialog circling around inside my head was that I'm fairly certain one of the reasons I do it this way is because I am confident in my methods. If I am confident in my methods, then doing it the way I do must give me the self-confidence that I am doing something good or right.

Are We Headed in the Right Direction?

It bears mentioning that I do not have the highest self-confidence when it comes to writing because I lack many of the proper writing skills that true wordsmiths might possess, but thankfully, gifted editors can take all the words my busy mind can spin out and skillfully piece them together into the final draft which you are reading now.

So, the one question I still needed to answer was how I felt about my own personal self-esteem. After all, I was, in fact, writing a book about the subject. Shouldn't I possess an unshakable self-esteem if I plan to write on the subject with the goal of supposedly showing others how to build their own unshakable self-esteem?

Well, to help me with my personal assessment, I recounted some things that stood out to me in my life that could affect my self-esteem and made a thought checklist:

Thought: I do question myself. At times, I ask myself the question, "Why am I here?"
My Thought Response: I feel that questioning yourself at times is healthy to do as long as it's done to build up and not tear down oneself.

Thought: I get upset with myself for the poor choices I have made in the past.
My Thought Response: Although many past mistakes were very painful, I have learned to *quick charge* and remind myself daily that the past is the past. I must let it go!

Thought: I hurt over lost relationships. I sometimes wonder, *was it my fault they chose to leave?*
My Thought Response: Life will bring pain at times. However, feeling pain does not need to be the end of the

world. In fact, I have found that life actually does go on. My friend, you will recover and grow stronger because of continuing on in spite of the hurt.

Thought: I've made many bad investment choices and squandered my money in the past.
My Thought Response: I realize that many people have lost hard-earned money in bad or misguided investments. I cannot allow those mistakes to hold me back from taking chances and pressing on.

Thought: My thinning hair bothers me at times. I want my thick full head of hair back from my younger days!
My Thought Response: Well, I don't like it, but I'm not alone. I do not need to look extremely far to see others with less hair than I have. Besides, it is only hair, and I should be much more concerned about who I am on the inside. Still, I would love to have my thick head of hair back from my younger years. Smile!

Thought: I have said things that hurt others about whom I cared deeply, yet I still hurt them badly and caused them great emotional pain.
My Thought Response: Well, this is another tough pill to swallow, but I must keep reminding myself that the past is the past! I can do better to appreciate and respect every person for who he or she is. I remind myself often that no one is perfect.

I could probably create a list three or four times the size of this one, detailing my many disappointments, downfalls, insecurities, failures, hurts, and so on. As you can see, life happens, and the consequences are not always perfect or pretty.

Considering the fact that I have so many faults and failures, how am I possibly qualified to write on such a delicate subject as self-esteem? How can I conceivably offer any real hope to my readers who have so graciously invested their time into reading my book when I obviously have had many issues in my own personal life as well?

I took some serious time to really pray and check myself on this subject, and with an overwhelming confidence, I knew I could write about self-esteem with passion. I have a strong belief that anyone can develop a healthy self-esteem—regardless of what life has thrown his or her way! With that belief in myself, I feel I can offer valuable input and tools to help you gain unshakable self-esteem!

I know I am far from perfect, and I realize I do not have all the answers or multiple degrees attached to my name, but what I can tell you is that I prayed about this book and continued to search my own self-esteem. I knew that with the Lord's guidance I could give you something of value. I have been there, and I continue to climb my mountain to victory. I can tell you there is HOPE, and you are worth it!

I believe that unshakable self-esteem takes a willingness to allow yourself to enjoy life's journey and not to worry about the final destination. In fact, the *quick-charge* concept about which I am so passionate has everything to do with continually thinking positive thoughts and seeking the Lord. If you have not read the original *Quick Charge Your Life* book, then perhaps you are not familiar with the concept of *quick charging your life*. The following is an excerpt from the introduction of my first book entitled *Quick Charge Your Life*:

The *quick-charge* life is about developing a personal relationship with the Lord and continually seeking Him to energize you with His power. It's about taking responsibility for your happiness by thinking positive thoughts—no matter what you may encounter in life. It's about learning to be calm and trusting the Lord during the storms in your life. It's about finding joy and blessing when you inspire others. It's also about generously giving of all that God has given you. In a nutshell, this book is an invitation for you to intentionally, deliberately and consciously change the way you think so that you might discover all the *quick-charge* outlets with which God surrounds you every single day of your life. The *quick-charge* concept will allow you to continually charge the power already living within you to move past your perceived limitations and boldly step into the life you were born to create.

When I read that paragraph again, I am reminded to *quick charge!* I thought, *why in the world should I think negatively and doubt myself?* I proclaimed to myself that I should not stop writing on this topic. I would be doing you (and myself, for that matter) a great disservice by putting this idea on the back burner simply because I may not be the world's foremost expert on self-esteem and self-confidence. You see, I live the *quick-charge* concept every single day of my life. My life is certainly not perfect, and I am as susceptible to pain, disappointment, and doubt as anyone else, but the *quick-charge* concept has given me tools to deal with anything and everything—both good and bad—that comes my way in life. Although I may not have a perfect life, I do feel I still have a tremendous self-worth, and I gain even more value when I write, speak, coach, and inspire others.

Just maybe I can offer you some hope and valuable perspectives to your life regarding self-esteem. After all, my mission is

Are We Headed in the Right Direction?

to embolden individuals to discover their uniqueness, realize their dreams and thrive in this lifetime. I have learned not to allow issues to bother me as much as they once did. I have learned to live the *quick-charge life* every single day and continually keep that charge going from the moment I awaken until the time I go to sleep at night.

Although I will always consider myself a work in progress, I do have a strong passion to help others. I can say with the utmost confidence that I am excited to dive into the topic of self-esteem in hopes that my findings will inspire at least ONE person to realize he or she has great value to offer this world and can become all that God created that one person to be. I hope that one person is you!

Learn it, live it, and inspire others! *Quick Charge Your Life! Unshakable Self-Esteem*

---

*Until you value yourself, you won't value your time.
Until you value your time, you
will not do anything with it.*
— M. Scott Peck

CHAPTER TWO

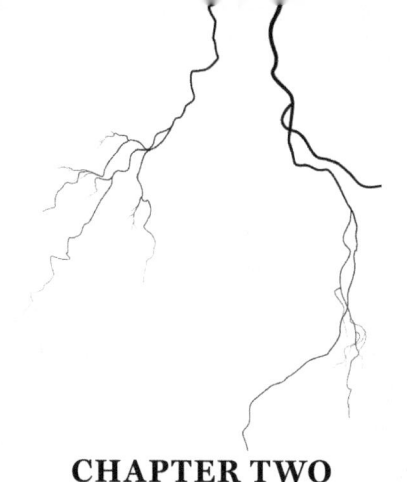

What Is Self-Esteem Anyway?

As I mentioned in the previous chapter, I had originally planned to write about self-confidence before settling on the idea to change the focus of this book to self-esteem. Once I decided to concentrate on self-esteem, I stumbled upon a great idea for a subtitle for this book or perhaps I should say the subtitle stumbled on me.

I had been considering several different powerful words and phrases to go along with self-esteem before deciding upon the word I ultimately chose—**unshakable**. In fact, this subtitle was born out of a situation I encountered while driving to an appointment.

Allow me to share a brief account of that epic discovery event. One day as I drove to one of my first appointments for the day, I started to feel somewhat anxious. As I have already mentioned in the introduction, I am writing this book while the entire WORLD is in the middle of the Covid-19 pandemic. Today's entry was written on April 7, 2020, to give you a time frame for my writing and thought process, assuming that months if not years have passed when you are reading this book.

Although I mentioned in the introduction that I am anticipating great things to come from the world pandemic crisis we are currently experiencing, I guess I was getting a bit overwhelmed as I thought about its impact on all those who do not have a faith in the Lord and who do not live the *quick-charge life*.

The crazy thing is, I had not felt these kinds of anxious feelings in a long while, but I quickly shifted my thoughts to positive affirmations that flooded out any fear. I instantly received a tremendous *quick charge* of energy from the Lord to press on! In that moment I felt **unshakable**!

I believe that my faith in the Lord has helped me to build an unshakable self-esteem. I have confidence in my worth and the value I have to offer others. I know that with the Lord's direction and power I can accomplish anything I set my mind to doing! Then I thought, *I want my readers to feel that same value within themselves. I want everyone who reads this book to develop an **unshakable** self-esteem!*

With that illustration in mind, I want to delve deeper into the meaning of self-esteem in order to help you build your own unshakable self-esteem.

In the last chapter I included a comparison of self-esteem and self-confidence along with a brief description of the meaning for each one. In this chapter, I would like to explore further into the meaning of self-esteem and look at other associated terms as well. For reference, the following definition of the noun *self-esteem* is from Dictionary.com:

- a realistic respect for or favorable impression of oneself; self-respect.
- an inordinately or exaggeratedly favorable impression of oneself.

What Is Self-Esteem Anyway?

Although this definition of self-esteem is based on the dictionary, I really feel the true meaning goes far deeper. In that respect, I want to look at this definition a little closer. What does it mean to have a "realistic respect for" or a "favorable impression of oneself"? After all, how does a person really measure an intangible like *respect*? I feel certain if we could all accurately measure what puts us on the "favorable" side of the scale, then perhaps we could simply aim for that mark and be good with ourselves.

What about measuring a "realistic respect"? What is even realistic in this world anymore? I personally think being realistic is limiting. I know many extraordinary people who, in my opinion, do unrealistic and unbelievable things every single day. This definition does not really help me evaluate my self-esteem.

Some additional synonyms I found when searching for the deeper meaning of self-esteem included self-assurance, self-image, self-love, self-worth, self-respect, and self-trust. Some additional associated words that attracted my attention were dignity and honor.

I found many other words as well, but I felt these that I have listed were most closely related or similar and could help paint a little clearer, broader picture for understanding self-esteem that the dictionary definition seemed to lack.

What lies behind us and what lies before us are tiny matters compared to what lies within us.
— Ralph Waldo Emerson

To gain a deeper understanding of self-esteem requires examining each of these words closer. I believe doing so will provide a "road map" to travel in discovering and developing our own personal definition of self-esteem.

Self-Assurance. How do you feel about your abilities? Being confident in your ability to do something might give you some confidence or satisfaction, but having confidence does not always bestow a high self-esteem on an individual.

Self-Image. How do you see yourself—mentally and/or physically? I feel this word is one of the closely related words to self-esteem that I found in my research, although self-esteem refers more to how you **feel** about yourself. I think how we **feel** about ourselves is much the same way we tend to **see** or perceive ourselves.

From a physical standpoint, I believe we often think we know how others see us, but we just might be wrong!

Consider two people with similar body types, hair color, and so forth. Because of their likenesses, you might think everyone would see them the same, but they might be viewed quite differently based completely on how they carry themselves. Also, the clothes they wear, their personalities, social status, and many other contributing factors will influence how they are viewed by others.

When you strip away all of those factors, then yes, they may look similar physically, but to a degree we all have the ability to change our looks. Of course, I am not talking about surgically altering one's body although many resort to those treatments to feel better about themselves.

Michael Jackson made the song, "Man in the Mirror" famous. The lyrics include the following:

And no message could have been any clearer.

If you want to make the world a better place.
Take a look at yourself, and then make a change.

As many already know, Michael continually tried to change his appearance and image until his tragic death. Michael Jackson seemingly had all the fame, talent, and fortune a person could imagine in life, yet he seemingly lacked a healthy self-image and/or self-esteem. Quite possibly his self-confidence and self-assurance in his abilities to entertain people through song and dance were much higher than his self-image.

Self-Love. This concept may be baffling for many to understand. Many people can seemingly love others but not themselves. I find one of the best ways to love myself is to perceive the concept that God loves me and created me in His image. I know He created me for a purpose, and He also created *you* for a purpose as well. We can love ourselves because God put tremendous care into creating each and every one of us.

So God created mankind in his own image,
in the image of God he created them;
male and female he created them.
— GENESIS 1:27 (NIV)

Self-Worth. Putting a value—high or low—on our life is also hard to comprehend. If you have a negative self-esteem, you likely feel worthless and insignificant. However, nothing could be farther from the truth. My friend, you have great value regardless of how you feel about yourself. You simply have yet to discover that value. Remember, if you are struggling with self-esteem, then your opinion of yourself is not a good measure or gauge of your self-worth.

As someone who has struggled with self-worth in the past, I can assure you that NO ONE is without great value. You can choose to increase your value every day. Although some may feel they have little-to-no value in this life, anyone can gradually turn around that belief by finding one positive value in his life.

I have great news! I believe I can give you some value right now. The very fact that you are reading this book adds value to your life. You are acting and searching for ways to find more direction and worth in your life by reading this book. You are already making an investment into your life's value!

Self-Respect. While conducting some research, I found the definition for *self-respect* is "a feeling that one is behaving with honor and dignity." I feel this interpretation impacts us at a personal level. Are you conducting yourself in private in a way that others would question? If so, you need to break free of those habits. You can start doing that today by purposing to live the *quick-charge life!*

Self-Trust. Do you believe in your abilities to make good decisions? We must make important decisions every day when it comes to our relationships, parenting, finances, and so forth. Many people do not trust themselves when it comes to making the right choices in life. We must realize that no one will ever make all the right calls, but we can make good decisions. Look at the positives and let go of the negatives.

You can't make decisions based on fear and the possibility of what might happen.
— MICHELLE OBAMA

Dignity. One definition of *dignity* says, "the state or quality of being worthy of honor or respect." If you have a low self-esteem, you likely do not feel like you deserve honor or respect. Perhaps this feeling was caused by a lack of respect you felt when you were a child. Maybe a tragic event or a bad decision in your life has left you feeling unworthy of honor. People who were close to you might have knowingly or even unknowingly treated you with little-to-no respect or abuse.

What Is Self-Esteem Anyway?

Don't let another person's poor opinion of you or his actions toward you define you. Only God's opinion matters. He believed you were worth dying for on the cross.

> *Remember always that you not only have the right to be an individual, you have an obligation to be one.*
> — ELEANOR ROOSEVELT

Honor. I would like to pose a question for you to consider: do you honor others? I feel that many people do not take the time to honor and appreciate those who add value to their lives. Perhaps I should say that far too often we forget to honor and appreciate others until it's too late, and they are gone. You can honor others by adding value to their life, and in so doing, you will surely add value to your own life as well.

I would also like you to ask yourself, "Do I honor me?" My friend, do you allow yourself the opportunity to build your self-esteem? Do you take "ME" time and purpose to add value to your life? You are currently reading this book, and the very fact that you possess a willingness to seek answers by reading this book in hopes of improving your self-esteem is proof enough that you have hope and value.

Learn it, live it, and inspire others! *Quick Charge Your Life! Unshakable Self-Esteem*

> *Self-care is never a selfish act; it is simply good stewardship of the only gift I have—the gift I was put on earth to offer to others.*
> — PARKER PALMER

CHAPTER THREE

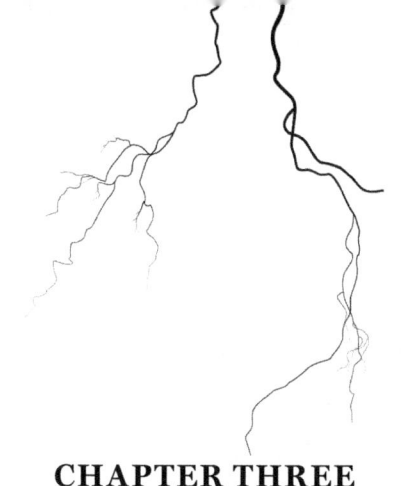

What Are You Missing?

Many people face physical challenges that simply will not allow them to live their life like others. That inability may be extremely difficult for some to process, but those who are faced with physical disabilities, imperfections or illness can overcome and handle the challenges they encounter head on and still create a life of inestimable value.

Many who face physical challenges often shy away from doing anything that exposes the difficulties they face on a daily basis. However, that very issue that brings them shame or frustration can be used to inspire others and add value to their life more than if they had no disability or imperfections at all.

If you have a physical complication that holds you back or makes life more challenging, then you need to realize and know that you have as much value to offer as anyone. If you are willing to work at developing a healthy self-esteem, you can use that newfound positive self-image to inspire anyone who also has a physical challenge as well. Not only that, you may inspire others who might struggle in life without any disadvantages.

A few people come to my mind whose stories can offer encouragement and inspiration to those who might be feeling they have nothing of value to offer to the world because of their struggles. Even if you do not have any physical challenges that hold you back, the following examples of a life redeemed should still inspire you.

Australian Evangelist, Nick Vujicic, "Life Without Limbs"

If God can use a man without arms and legs to be His hands and feet, then He will certainly use any willing heart!

– Nick Vujicic

The following excerpt is from Nick's website: *Meet Nicholas Vujicic (pronounced VOO-yee-cheech). Imagine getting through your busy day without hands or legs. Picture your life without the ability to walk, care for your basic needs, or even embrace those you love.*

I do not know Nick personally, but I have watched him speak online, and I have heard him interviewed on podcasts. If you are not familiar with who he is, you would do yourself a favor by checking out his website. I can tell you he is full of life.

He shares about dealing with depression as a young child while growing up. I am sure he has his good days and bad days even now—just like anyone else, but he has found a way to create great value in his life and share that value with others. Nick shares on his site that the victory over his struggles, as well as his strength and passion for life today, can be credited to his faith in God.

What Are You Missing?

I cannot emphasis enough exactly how powerful and loving our Heavenly Father is. I know it may seem difficult to process at times if you are someone like Nick who seemingly did not get a "fair deal" in life, but he has accepted his physical challenge and has created a life of great value.

I feel certain he might wish he had the opportunity to live a normal life with both his legs and arms, but he has learned to build his self-esteem and self-image on the foundation of the Lord—not on human expectations or perceptions. Because of his passion and drive in life, he is in great demand as a speaker, and God is using him to inspire millions around the world who seek hope.

As I was writing these paragraphs about him, I was thinking about my own life. *How could I possibly ever feel less about myself when I have so much for which to be thankful?* I can do anything I want for myself without any need to ask for or require assistance with everyday tasks in life. I also thought, *how can anyone who has the ability to care for himself, a privilege that Nick was denied, possibly even think about complaining about his life?*

Then I stopped and thought, *what are some of my own illnesses or potential disabilities?* In the past, I used to struggle with panic attacks and anxiety. Certainly, I recognize the fact that having a panic attack or anxiety does not begin to compare to having no legs or arms. However, at one point in my life, panic attacks literally kept me from using my own arms and legs to venture outside of my own home. When I gave those episodes to the Lord, He helped me overcome my fears. Still, I realize the possibility of my anxiety popping up or having a panic attack will always be in my record book of life. I work hard not to allow them to keep me from being all that God created me to be.

As I have mentioned, Nick is in great demand as a speaker, and God is using him to inspire millions of people all around the world. He has used what he has, or perhaps I should say, he has used what he does *not* have to inspire millions of people to live life with passion.

I have wondered if he had his legs and arms, would he still have the same unshakable self-esteem and drive he now possesses. I wonder what impact he would have on the world had he been born with all of his extremities. Obviously, I have no way to answer this hypothetical question. Perhaps his belief in himself would have been the same whether or not he had been born with limbs. Perhaps he would have done even more... What we do know is that he has taken what he has and has built it into a life of passion! His willingness to share his story of faith in God and the love and belief of his family has placed him in a ministry to change lives.

Man cannot discover new oceans unless he has the courage to lose sight of the shore.
– ANDRE GIDE

Clay Dyer, Professional Sport Bass Fisherman

Clay Dyer, much like Nick, was also born without legs and his left arm. He does have a partial right arm, but for the most part, doing everyday tasks would be extremely difficult for him to perform as well. In spite of his physical limitations, Clay has made his life about inspiring others. Clay's motto for life is *"If I can, you can."*

I do not have the pleasure of knowing Clay personally, but we do share a common interest of bass fishing. In fact, he has used the Pro Bass Tournament Fishing tour as his platform to inspire others to enjoy the life they have regardless of any physical challenges they might have.

One of my greatest joys in life happens to be bass fishing with my son Andrew. We have fished in bass tournaments together since he was a young boy, and we have one exclusive tournament in which we fish every year. That tournament is more like Christmas morning for us when it comes around each year in May!

I know firsthand how difficult it can be to fish for bass even with both of my legs and arms. I still have difficulties at times, so I cannot imagine what fishing is like for Clay. I have watched him fishing on TV, and I have studied his unusual technique. He tucks his pole under his chin for support, reels with the small nub of his arm, and lands bass after bass! I have watched him tie and bait his hooks with his mouth. He is an amazing inspiration and has such an upbeat attitude and unshakable self-esteem. He deals with so much more than most to enjoy a sport I can enjoy without even thinking twice about how I will reel in the fish, set the hook, bait my hook or any of the myriad of actions one must do to be a good bass fisherman.

Clay also credits his faith in the Lord for giving him the strength to do what he does. You would think Clay and Nick would be angry at God for their physical challenges, but they have allowed their lives to be witnesses to the power the Lord has instilled within them to use their lives for good—no matter how difficult the circumstances.

The physical challenges you might have (or NOT have) should never be an excuse for holding you back. You simply need to see the person in you who can add great value to others. The challenges you have may not even be physical or visible. You might have imperfections and difficulties in your life that have held you back like the panic attacks I once allowed in my life.

Many people may be disregarded or judged in some circles for their disabilities, imperfections, and or failures in the past, but I am certain the Lord can use them in plenty of circles in spite of their imperfections. Yes, my friend, I absolutely believe you have every bit as much value as anyone no matter the challenges you face.

Bethany Hamilton, Professional Surfer

Bethany was a thirteen-year-old top amateur surfer who was a force to be reckoned with, but all that changed in 2003 when she was attacked by a fourteen-foot tiger shark in Kauai, Hawaii.

For most people, a devasting event like that would likely end their surfing career and could very easily damage one's self-image. In fact, an incident like this shark attack would most likely plummet the person's self-esteem to the lowest levels. However, Bethany had a different self-image of herself. She still saw herself as a professional surfer who only needed to readjust the way she surfed.

I recently watched a documentary on her, and she beautifully illustrated how she views herself. She also shared how any person should see himself or herself regardless of what issues—the loss of a limb, disfiguring scars, life issues or anything else that makes life more challenging—the person may need to resolve in life.

Bethany chose a rose as her focus. She shared that not all roses are red nor perfect, but all roses have something **beautiful** about them! Remove a few of the petals, and the rose is still gorgeous. In the same way, each one of us is a beautiful

What Are You Missing?

rose—unique, colorful, growing, changing, and reflecting the life that God has given us. The petals falling off can resemble different issues in our lives, i.e., the loss of a limb, an eating disorder, or even family pain.

Hearing her share this incredible word picture of how we should all view our lives as a rose was a *quick-charge* moment for me. The thought of viewing our lives as a rose will be encased in my mind and last a lifetime in my storage bank of thoughts to glean from when I need a *quick charge* to boost my self-esteem and self-image. Some "petals" of your life may have fallen off or even been pulled off by others, yet you are still a beautiful rose.

Your life will always remain a beautiful rose—even as petals fall off. Perhaps you have lost some of your limbs or perhaps you were born without certain extremities or maybe you deal with other issues in life—your weight, your height, physical scars, or other bodily *deformities*. Maybe you have deep pain from terrible abuse as a child or as a battered spouse. Whatever you view as bad, ugly, irreversible, and unrepairable in your life, you need to hold tight to Bethany's message of seeing yourself as a beautiful rose!

Learn it, live it, and inspire others! *Quick Charge Your Life! Unshakable Self-Esteem*

Anger, resentment and jealousy doesn't change the heart of others; it only changes yours.

– SHANNON ALDER

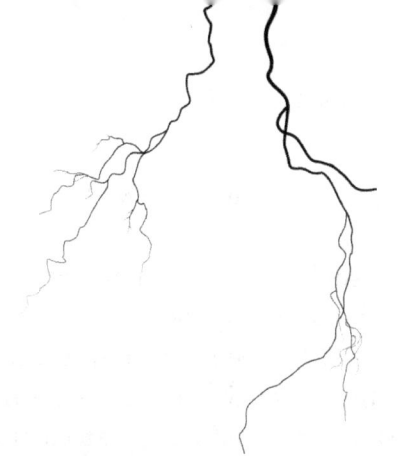

CHAPTER FOUR

Abused and Broken

Part One

The previous chapter focused primarily on how people who have disabilities, imperfections, and illnesses can allow them to either make or break them when it comes to their self-image or self-esteem. The examples in the chapter revealed how you can be up against all odds of any hope for success based on the mere physical challenges you may face in life. Yet you can still learn to value yourself and focus on what you do have instead of what you don't and create a life of inestimable value—like Nick, Clay, and Bethany have done in their own personal lives. I love Clay's motto for life: *"If I can, you can."*

You are loved just for being who you are, just for existing. You don't have to do anything to earn it. Your shortcomings, your lack of self-esteem, physical perfection, or social and economic success—none of that matters. No one can take this love away from you, and it will always be here.

– Ram Dass

In this chapter and the next, I want to address another type of disability, imperfection, and illness that can be very crippling to person's self-esteem. In fact, these particular challenges often unfairly shape how and why a person develops an extremely low self-esteem. The downward spiral usually continues, and the person lives a broken life until finding the courage to see that a new self-image can empower him or her to build unshakable self-esteem.

The topic I am choosing to address in this chapter is deeply sensitive and one I will approach with great care and love. This chapter will deal with those who have been abused, bullied, and/or tormented by others. The mental torment and physical abuse that some people have been subjected to can bring incredible pain, both mental and physical scars, and a myriad of other emotional issues that are almost unfathomable to comprehend. I feel sure some who are reading this book are still trapped in an abusive situation, desperately searching for hope. For anyone who suffers or has ever suffered abuse, please know there is a way to build unshakable self-esteem and create a life of incredible value.

I have prayed for anyone who may be traumatized by any of the stories I will share in this chapter or the next. My prayer is also in regard to the sensitivity of any discussion about this topic. I realize abuse can bring up terrible memories for some, but I feel addressing this subject is essential and vital in the hopes that it will bring healing and hope to someone seeking to build an unshakable self-esteem. I believe that your being able to see the incredible value you possess by redeeming any trauma and abuse you may have suffered in your life will inspire you to move past your perceived limitations and boldly step into the life you were born to create!

Please say the following prayer with me, and if it does not directly pertain to you, may I ask you to pray for someone else who has suffered or is presently suffering. We may not even know who this prayer will bless.

> *Lord, I ask that You will bring peace and comfort right now to those who suffer from the effects of abuse and trauma. Often, no explanation is feasible for the trauma and abuse that has been inflicted on one of Your children, as we are all your precious sons and daughters. Lord, I know You are able to heal anyone who asks. I pray that You will create unshakable self-esteem in those who call upon Your name. I ask that You show Your love and grace to anyone who suffers from past abuse and trauma or to anyone who is seeking a way out of a current abusive situation. I ask that You bring comfort and peace as they read the accounts that follow and speak love and hope into their lives! In Jesus' name. Amen.*

Let the journey toward hope and healing begin...

I love traveling on short getaways to the Oregon coast near where I live. I always look forward to traveling with great anticipation as I have the most incredible times. I love meeting new people along the way, taking in all the beautiful scenery, and looking forward to each new day and adventure that awaits me.

On one particular coastal adventure, I was exposed to a situation that I had never before experienced in my entire life. I pray I will never encounter circumstances like this situation again. I feel certain you will quickly understand why what

I encountered shook me to my core, and thus, this chapter came about.

I had finished eating dinner at a favorite local restaurant around 6:30 p.m. and had returned to my hotel room. I started to watch a television program, but a few minutes later, I thought I could hear some strange sounds coming from the room next to me. I turned down the TV to listen, and to my shock and horror, I could hear a man screaming loudly and berating a woman in the adjacent room. I could immediately tell that what I was hearing was not a *normal* husband/wife spat or quarrel.

I had absolutely no idea what the relationship was between this couple, but regardless, I could tell I was hearing a heated encounter. I could not tell whether or not he was physically abusing her, but he was definitely verbally and emotionally abusing her to a degree I had never heard before in my life. He repeatedly screamed at her in a guttural angry voice, asking her why she was such a disgusting human being and why she did this and that—the reason for his need to yell at the top of his lungs...

Each time he would ask her a question, I could tell she was trying to answer meekly, but he would immediately cut her off and scream profane disgusting words at her again. Then he would ask her the same questions repeatedly. He was spewing vile hatred toward her as if she were the scum of the earth. His language could only be described as issuing demonic threats and tormenting words. Of course, I could not see her, but I could hear her weak voice trembling in fear as she attempted to answer him.

The rooms, of course, were all locked, so I had no way to gain access to their room. My heart was racing a million miles an hour as I tried to figure out a way to help this poor woman. I felt she seemed to be in grave danger of a violent physical attack.

About that time the security guards came rushing down the hallway and started banging on the door to gain access to the room. Even though the guards were literally standing right outside the door and demanding he open the door, the bully ignored them and continued to berate this woman. I was afraid he might even have a gun and start shooting. To say I was experiencing one of the most intense and terrifying moments of my life would be an understatement.

I kept wondering, *why in the world won't these guards break down the door and force their way inside to put an end to this horrible situation?* I wanted to bust down the door myself and stop this unearthly outbreak immediately. However, the guards were much calmer and more collected about the whole situation than I was. I wondered, *are they acting like this because they really don't care about the situation? Perhaps they did not have proper training in an encounter like this.*

Anyway, regardless of my concerns and suggestions, the guards continued to talk calmly to the man, demanding he open the door and let them come inside. This horrible exchange continued for at least five more minutes until the man finally agreed to open the door and let the guards inside.

After the guards entered the room, it sounded to me like they took the woman aside to determine if she had any physical wounds. After they had determined the woman had not been physically harmed, they visited with the couple for a while and talked about what had been happening and possible resolutions. I heard them ask the woman, "Are you going to be okay?" Of course, she answered, "Yes." What else could she say with this maniac sitting right there in the room with her? *No! She is not going to be okay!* I thought to myself!

Then to my amazement, the guards wished the couple a good evening and left. *What? I mean how could they possibly leave this poor woman in the same room with this monster?* Well, shortly after the guards left, I could hear the man apologizing to her and saying, "I love you." He began calling her "Baby" and "Sweetie." *I mean seriously?*

They seemed to resolve their issues quickly, which was apparently over money she had spent earlier that day. Yes, the walls were so paper thin, I could hear everything discussed or rather screamed. After hearing them talk for a few minutes, I heard him say, "Let's go out to dinner," and they left their room to go out.

They returned to their room about an hour later, and to my amazement, they were laughing together and saying sweet things to one another—as if nothing had ever happened. I was still numb with emotion and stunned in disbelief that she could even be having a conversation with this horrible excuse for a man. I was praying for this poor woman and for the man as well to find help. I am almost certain this incident was probably not the first time he had clashed with her in this type of exchange. Sadly, I am fairly sure it wouldn't be the last. I pray that this couple found help for their issues.

Now I want to address the guards' reactions to this incident… I had to wonder what the deal was. First off, I guess defusing this incident was nothing new for them at all. Unfortunately, they deal with these types of incidents on a weekly basis, and apparently, even multiple times per week during peak seasons. If they were to break down every door (like I wanted to do) for outbursts like the one I overheard, probably half the doors in that hotel complex would need repair at some point.

Then I wondered, *why did the guards simply walk away?* I mean, they could clearly hear the same disgusting human being on the other side of the door as I could. Why did they not arrest him? Because of his eventual compliance in letting them come into the room, they did not need to arrest him. Again, they would be arresting guests all the time for unfortunate incidents if they were to arrest someone every time they defused a heated domestic dispute outbreak. Furthermore, I guess she did not wish to press charges against him, so they had to let the matter drop.

These revelations really shook me to the core. I am far from perfect, and I will admit that I have been in some arguments with a spouse or former girlfriend. I have also been guilty of being far too judgmental and insensitive toward women about whom I cared in the past. I know I hurt them deeply, and I wish I could take it all back, but I have never screamed profanities or treated a woman (or anyone for that matter) like I heard that man treat a woman in the room next to mine that night.

However, as I learned that night, apparently, these are regular encounters for some people. What I heard coming from that room was so vile and truly beyond anything I have ever experienced or heard in my entire life. He treated her as if she was not even a human being, and yet, an hour later they were making up and laughing together. How could this possibly be? How could she allow this behavior to continue?

Perhaps this story sounds all too familiar for someone reading this account. I am certain that her self-image and self-esteem were shattered. I am also certain she felt there was no way out, so she was making the best of what seemed to be a bad situation.

Unfortunately, as I have learned in my research on this topic, it would appear that accepting her situation in life is really not all that uncommon. Many women and some men as well suffer this kind of horrific abusive torment on a regular basis and often stay trapped in these horrible cycles of violent attacks—both verbally and physically—for years.

If you have been abused in anyway, please know you are not alone. I pray you will see yourself as lovely as Bethany Hamilton's rose. Although you have had petals picked and torn from your life from domestic abuse, you are still a beautiful rose. You deserve to be treated with respect and dignity. No one deserves to be treated the way I heard this woman treated.

I would like to close this chapter with a thought that the Lord gave me as I was praying. We all have a choice on how we will handle the burdens, mistakes, disappointments, pain, and trauma that pile up and block us from many things in our lives. We can either allow all of those stresses, burdens, mistakes, disappointments, trauma, and pain in our lives to pile up and impede our life's journey, effectively burying our dreams and hopes OR we can see them simply as obstacles that can be moved aside as we climb to the top of our mountain.

Learn it, live it, and inspire others! *Quick Charge Your Life! Unshakable Self-Esteem*

Abuse is never deserved; it is an exploitation of innocence and physical disadvantage, which is perceived as an opportunity by the abuser.
– LORRAINE NILON

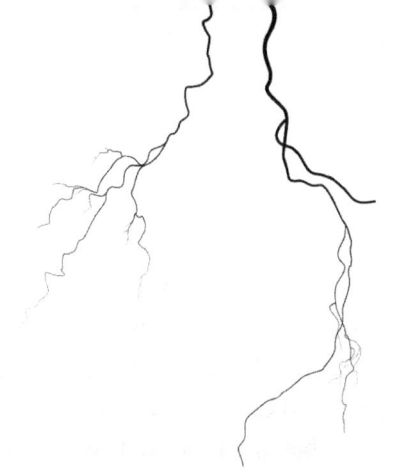

CHAPTER FIVE

Abused and Broken

Part Two

I have changed the names of the people in the following true accounts that I have either read about or watched on television programs.

Jill

On a television program about human trafficking several years ago, I heard Jill tell her story of being kidnapped at a young age, sold into slavery, and eventually rescued. During much of her time spent in captivity, she was housed in a cage, only released to perform deviant sexual acts for her captor or to travel with him.

Her life spent in captivity contributed to her deception about her self-esteem and value in life as her captor would often take her on lavish vacations. On these trips, he would buy her expensive clothes and treat her to expensive meals as they stayed in luxury hotels around the world. His acts against her were egregious, and at times, she should have felt like she was worth no more than an animal; however, she was blinded by this strange world and bizarre treatment.

Sadly, after her rescue, Jill felt she should return to her abuser because she no longer knew how to live normal life and function in society. Jill had grown so accustomed to the degrading lifestyle and abuse that she felt her only value was to return to his horrible mistreatment. When questioned about this desire by the program host, she reasoned that her captor had treated her decently the times they had travelled together. Unfortunately, Jill could not see that the abuse and torment to which he had been subjecting her was NOT treating her well. She had devalued herself to the point that she now accepted his mistreatment as acceptable behavior.

Sadly, whether you were a victim of human trafficking or spousal abuse as addressed in the previous chapter or any other type or mistreatment of this kind where you were degraded and forced to live a certain lifestyle, you must realize that your value should not be based on the opinion or treatment of others. You do not need to try to convince yourself that being mistreated is accepted. You have much more value and worth than you will ever realize! You have reason to hope!

Let me stress that NO ONE—no man or woman ever deserves to be devalued in the way Jill was. Sadly, Jill, like many others, had no concept of what a healthy self-image looked like. The only worth she found was in allowing someone to control and abuse her. I wish I could tell you what came of Jill's life, but I do not know what she decided to do after the show aired. I do know she was offered counseling and assistance, and I pray she accepted the producer's offer and is free from that man's control today, but I cannot say for certain.

Sadly, I am sure far more Jills are in the world than anyone cares to realize. Chances are they could be in our own backyard. I have a good friend named Dan whose wife, Nita Belles, has dedicated her life to helping young woman trapped in human trafficking. She authored the book, *In Our Backyard: Human Trafficking in America and What We Can Do to Stop It*. I would suggest you pick up a copy if you are unaware of how real this issue is.

Jackie

Jackie was only thirteen years old when her uncle slipped into her bedroom and raped her. His deplorable attacks continued for years. As Jackie told her story in a television interview, she shared that his first few visits were shocking, and she was not sure what to think or say. However, she recounted that each time became easier to accept because he "loved" her—at least that was the lie he repeatedly told her. Unfortunately for Jackie, she believed him.

Anyone with a sound mind would recognize this demented man needed help, and she was unfortunately a victim of egregious child abuse. Sadly, these abusive acts perpetrated by family members and friends happen around the world every day. This type of abuse also knows no gender.

Physical, verbal, and sexual abuse have affected my family's life as well. Unfortunately, most people have either personally been a victim of some form of abuse or have someone in their family who has experienced it at some point in his or her life. Thus, I felt it important to include these accounts in the book with the hope of bringing some perspective to those who may have never dealt with such devaluing actions. I also hope to bring healing to those who have suffered from this tragic injustice in their own life.

If you have been a victim of abuse, I want you to see yourself shoving aside all of that pain, anger, questions, and confusion you might have from those paralyzing events in your life as you continue to climb your life's mountain to victory.

Sadly, millions of people around the world have been victims of multiple types of abuses. To bring this subject into chilling perspective, by the time you finish reading this chapter alone, several more innocent children and adults alike will have fallen prey to some form of physical, verbal, and/or sexual abuse for the first time in their lives. This harsh reality is tough to understand, but the healing comes when the victim realizes that his or her value is far beyond any abuse ever suffered. My friend, you can climb your mountain and rise above it!

Many passionate, successful, and beautiful people in this world have suffered similar abuses as you may have endured, but they have chosen to use their hurts as inspiration to climb to the top of their life's mountain. You can do the same when you begin to see your pain as nothing more than another obstacle that can be moved aside as you scale your mountain and climb higher! I challenge you to climb your mountain, put aside your pain and trauma as if it were a boulder or another obstacle, and form a picture in your mind of seeing yourself standing at the top of your mountain. Please don't allow your pain and torment at the hands of another to bury you.

Bullying

In today's world, we often communicate through social media outlets. People post comments telling about the events going on in life and sometimes share pictures and videos with others online. This sharing can be both good and bad. One of the issues with so much online interaction is that of bullying

Abused and Broken

and how people can be pushed to the point of even taking their own lives. Bullying is another type of abuse that can affect a person's self-esteem.

Of course, this same bullying can be carried over into personal interactions offline as well. Bullying has currently become an exceedingly serious problem among teens and even elementary-age children in our school systems across America. Tragic stories are revealed on news stations about a young person taking his life as the direct result of being bullied by classmates.

Unfortunately, bullying will probably never be completely eliminated, but victims of this type of abuse can overcome the affects it has on their self-esteem. Chances are the person or people who have inflicted this pain on others are much worse off than their victims. The likelihood that they have also been a victim of the same type of abuse at some point in their own life and never dealt with it properly is very real. For the most part, bullies are simply acting in revenge toward their victims. This knowledge does not make bullying right or easier to endure but having an understanding of the situation can bring some answers and perspective. I also want the victims of bullying to envision the analogy of the rose and to know that no matter how beaten down they may feel, they are still beautiful roses. I am reminded of a story I read once about a boy who was bullied.

A Boy Named Kyle

One day, when I was a freshman in high school, I saw a kid from my class walking home from school. His name was Kyle. It looked like he was carrying all of his books. I thought to myself, *why would anyone bring home all his books on a Friday? He must really be a nerd.* I had quite a weekend planned with parties and a football game with my friend on Saturday afternoon, so I shrugged my shoulders and went on. As I continued walking, I saw a bunch of kids running toward him. They ran at him, knocked all of his books out of his arms and tripped him so he landed in the dirt. His glasses went flying, and I saw them land in the grass about ten feet from him. He looked up, and I saw this terrible sadness in his eyes. My heart went out to him. So, I jogged over to him, and as he crawled around looking for his glasses, I saw a tear in his eye.

As I handed him his glasses, I said, "Those guys are jerks. They really should get lives."

He looked at me and said, "Hey, thanks!" There was a big smile on his face. It was one of those smiles that showed real gratitude.

I helped him pick up his books and asked him where he lived. As it turned out, he lived near me, so I asked him why I had never seen him before. He said he had gone to private school before now. I would have never hung out with a private school kid before.

We talked all the way home, and I carried his books. He turned out to be a pretty cool kid. When I asked him if he wanted to play football on Saturday with my friends and me, he said "Yes." We hung all weekend, and the more I got to know Kyle, the more I liked him. And my friends thought the same of him.

Monday morning came, and there was Kyle with the huge stack of books again. I stopped him and said, "Boy, you are gonna really build some serious muscles with this pile of books every day!" He just laughed and handed me half the books. Over the next four years, Kyle and I became best friends. When we were seniors, we began to think about college. Kyle decided on Georgetown, and I was going to Duke. I knew that we would always be friends and that the smiles would never be a problem. He was going to be a doctor, and I was going for business on a football scholarship. Kyle was valedictorian of our class.

I teased him all the time about being a nerd. He had to prepare a speech for graduation. I was so glad it wasn't me having to get up there and speak.

On Graduation day, I saw Kyle. He looked great. He was one of those guys who really found himself during high school. He had filled out and actually looked good in glasses. He had more dates than me, and all the girls loved him! Sometimes I was jealous.

Today was one of those days. I could see that he was nervous about his speech. So, I smacked him on the back and said, "Hey, big guy, you'll be great!"

He looked at me with one of those really grateful looks and smiled. "Thanks," he said.

As he started his speech, he cleared his throat. "Graduation is a time to thank those who helped you make it through those tough years—your parents, your teachers, your siblings, maybe a coach...but mostly your friends. I am here to tell all of you that being a friend to someone is the best gift you can give the person. I am going to tell you a story."

I just stared at my friend with disbelief as he told the story of the first day we met. He had planned to kill himself over the weekend. He talked of how he had cleaned out his locker so his mom wouldn't have to do it later and was carrying his stuff home. He looked hard at me and smiled. "Thankfully, I was saved. My friend saved me from doing the unspeakable." I heard the gasp go through the crowd as this handsome, popular boy told us all about his weakest moment.

I saw his mom and dad looking at me and smiling that same grateful smile. Not until that moment did I realize its depth.

Never underestimate the power of your actions. With one small gesture you can change a person's life. For better or for worse. God puts us all in each other's lives to impact one another in some way. Look for God in others.

Regardless of how others make you feel, you possess the power to believe in yourself and climb your mountain. No one can take that power from you. You can build an *unshakable self-esteem* and see yourself standing at the top of your mountain regardless of what other people may say about you or how they treat you.

I know that one of the main issues people of abuse often face is personal **guilt** and **self-blame**. The guilt or blame can be deafening to the truth. You continue to ask yourself how or why you ended up in the situation in the first place. In the case of Jill, I feel sure she would question why she was chosen to become a victim of human trafficking and why she was the one who was captured and sold into such a degrading lifestyle.

I feel sure that Jackie felt embarrassed and confused as to what and why her uncle chose to put her in an incestuous relationship.

I can only imagine that spouses who find themselves in abusive relationships must feel so lost and so ashamed of their lot in life.

Some victims of abuse might wonder what THEY did wrong for their relationship to deteriorate into an abusive one. Perhaps they even repeat this pattern of choosing abusive partners and wonder why they can't seem to choose a good partner to love them.

Abused and Broken

Let me assure you that guilt and shame have no place in your life. You have full control of your personal opinion of yourself regardless of the abuses you have been endured. I am in no way saying it's fair, easy, or acceptable by any means because abuse is never acceptable under any conditions. What I am saying is regardless of whatever negative images you see and believe about yourself, you can choose to turn that image into something beautiful—like a rose.

You can lift up your head and know that you did nothing to deserve the horrible abuses you have experienced. You can try to reason all you want in order to try and ease the pain, but you do not need to reason. You are not unworthy; God says you have incredible value! You are a beautiful rose! You can and will climb to the top of your life's mountain!

An unknown author wrote a poem titled "The Chosen Vessel" which tells how God searches for a vessel to use.

"Take me," cried the gold one, "I'm shiny and bright,
I'm of great value and I do things exactly right."

However, the gold one isn't chosen, and the poem explains why God bypasses the gold, and then the silver, brass, crystal, and wooden urns to make a different choice:

Then the master looked down and saw a vessel of clay.
Empty and now broken, it helplessly lay.
No hope had the vessel that the Master might choose,
To cleanse, and to make whole, to fill and to use.

"Ah! Now this is the vessel I've been hoping to find.
I'll mend it and use it and make it mine."

Learn it, live it, and inspire others! *Quick Charge Your Life! Unshakable Self-Esteem*

You can recognize survivors of abuse by their courage. When silence is so very inviting, they step forward and share their truth so others know they aren't alone.

– Jeanne McElvaney

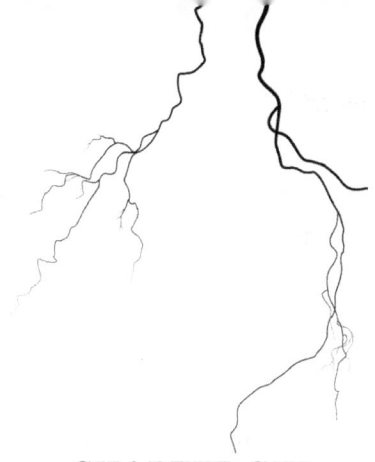

CHAPTER SIX

Is It Pride or Healthy Self-Esteem?

Whether or not you have ever been a victim of abuse and have no concept of the pain, the last couple of chapters may have been difficult ones for some readers as they were reminded of the horrific experiences they have had to endure. I feel sure for many who have experienced any type of abuse, the chapters may have stirred some painful memories locked deep within. Perhaps their self-esteem has been left shattered by those tragic events.

This chapter will leave those painful subjects and instead address a very different side of self-esteem. Many people would laugh at the notion that they struggle with a low self-esteem. Some people can overcompensate or become so overly confident in who they are to the point that not only do they not believe they have low self-esteem, they will even tell you how great they are doing.

If you see anything in yourself which may make you proud, look a little further, and you will find enough to make you humble.

– WELLINS CALCOTT

Overly confident people often have an extremely high opinion of themselves and feel they are a gift to all. In reality, they may be overcompensating for issues in their past. Perhaps a parent, a teacher or another authority figure told them they were no good, worthless, and would never be anybody profitable.

This labeling, of course, could fall into the abuse and trauma topic already addressed, but instead of seeking healing and learning how to find true value, they convinced themselves they were valuable to the point of actually becoming prideful or conceited. A past issue or some former trauma resulted in their overcompensating for their low self-esteem.

But at some point, they crossed the line, and now their so-called self-esteem is clouding their image of themselves, giving them a false identity. They may have an exceedingly high self-image of themselves, which can be both healthy and negative—if they are not careful. Perhaps they work out at the gym often and have sculpted their body to near perfection in their eyes.

Not crossing the line into a prideful state for those who are extremely confident in certain aspects of their life and in who they are can be like walking a tightrope—precarious and risky. For people to value who they are and have a strong self-image is wonderful. But we must always check ourselves to be certain we do not become prideful or conceited in our abilities and or accomplishments.

Pride, like the magnet, constantly points to one object, self; but unlike the magnet, it has no attractive pole, but at all points repels.
– CHARLES CALEB COLTON

Is It Pride or Healthy Self-Esteem?

I happen to be an avid Oregon Duck fan. I especially love watching the Oregon women's basketball team and have been a season ticket holder since 2018. I had the unbelievable opportunity to watch Sabrina Ionescu, Ruthy Hebard, Satou Sabally and the rest of those incredible young ladies play basketball at an extraordinarily high level. Unfortunately, the worldwide coronavirus pandemic in 2020 spoiled their chances to seek a national championship. Duck fans will never know if the team could have won it all. Nonetheless, their talent and grace on the court was undeniable, but what made me such a huge fan was their playful personalities and enthusiasm displayed toward one another and their fans.

Yes, they knew they were good. Yes, they may have even been somewhat overconfident at times, but I truly do believe that at the core of those ladies was great humility for the opportunity and skills they possessed on the court. I feel sure some of those women may have struggled with their self-esteem and self-confidence, but their playing as a team never seemed prideful. They knew they were good, but their abilities never seemed boastful or cocky.

My friend, how do you measure your high self-esteem or self-image to make certain you are not so confident in who you are that it becomes prideful?

Perhaps this illustration from my own life might shed some light on how to check for pride in yourself. I struggled with my own self-esteem and pride for many years until I learned to speak positive affirmations into my life and *quick charge* on a regular basis. I can speak passionately about this *quick-charge* topic! I am researching and writing this chapter in hopes that not only will my takeaway possibly shed even more light on the topic for me personally, but that it would embolden you to discover your uniqueness, realize your dreams and thrive in this lifetime.

I do not think that being proud of yourself or the fact that you are proud of your accomplishments is bad. However, for me personally, I knew I had to be careful not to cross a definite line and allow myself to become too proud of what I had accomplished in life.

> *Be strong, but not rude; be kind, but not weak; be bold, but not bully; be thoughtful, but not lazy; be humble, but not timid; be proud, but not arrogant; have humor, but without folly.*
> – Jim Rohn

Whenever I am recounting my personal successes or events in my life to someone else, I can definitely feel when I am crossing the line and have evolved into a bragging or prideful state. At this point, I am shining the light on myself rather than sharing a blessing in my life in hopes it would shine the light on others to bring value to their lives.

Where does the light shine when you are sharing about something you have done or accomplished in life with others? If the light is shining on you, then it is pride. If the light is shining on your subjects, then what God has allowed you to accomplish can inspire others.

I believe we all have a so-called internal "smoke detector" inside of us. What do I mean? I believe people can often share with others about accomplishments and or successes they may have experienced, but a fire can begin to rage inside when they go overboard.

Perhaps you start sharing about meeting someone famous or you tell others about business accomplishments that brought

Is It Pride or Healthy Self-Esteem?

you some acclaim. I think sharing with excitement and passion because you are excited for what God has enabled you to do is good. When sharing with passion, enthusiasm and gratefulness about accomplishments or big events in your life allows you to inspire others—as long as your reasons for sharing are to encourage or inspire others. The light is shining on them and not on you. So, that little internal smoke detector simply blinks to remind you that the battery is charged, but there is no smoke to detect, so you're good.

When I am speaking or talking to a new acquittance, I might share about how incredibly blessed and grateful I am to be living the *quick-charge life* I am living now. I might share about some famous entertainers I have had the privilege of meeting, but when I start sharing about my accomplishments, I must remember the purpose for which I am sharing them. If I am not careful, I can turn the spotlight on myself and away from the ones I was intending to inspire.

When I have told my story for the pure gratification of just wanting to hear the story again, I can usually sense that I am going off course, and not sharing for anyone's benefit other than my own. These are the times when the smoke starts to smolder, and I set off the internal smoke detector.

Once I became aware of this shortcoming in my personal life, I often heard the detector loud and clear and caught myself. In those instances, I quickly put out the flame. Yes, when I got off track and my pride would sneak up on me, I quickly had to put out the flame. Nonetheless, I had once again set off the alarm.

Indeed, I still set off the smoke alarm at times, and I am generally good about putting out the fire very quickly and turning off the alarm. I have learned that I must stay aware when I am sharing about personal successes that I have attained in life so that I am not prideful. I do not have to look far to find others who have achieved far greater things than I ever have or ever will accomplish.

I have learned to tell when the light is shining on me and when I am shining the light in the right direction to allow the blessing to inspire others.

I do hope that whenever you are sharing your life's successes with someone else that you realize that God has entrusted you with something very precious. We all must be extremely careful to handle His blessings in our lives with grace and humility in order to be certain that we use our gifts and talents to inspire others—not shine the light on ourselves.

Learn it, live it, and inspire others! *Quick Charge Your Life! Unshakable Self-Esteem*

Pride goes before a fall, they say, and yet we often find, the folks who throw all pride away most often fall behind.

– EDGAR GUEST

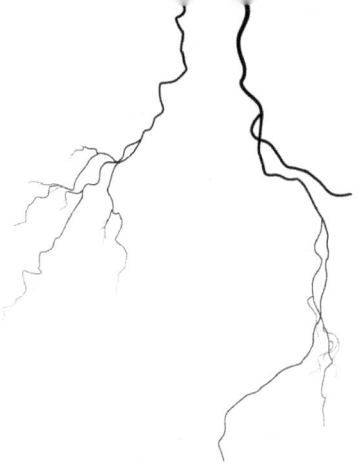

CHAPTER SEVEN

The Beginning Pages of Life

Up to this point, I have primarily addressed the subject of building our own self-esteem. However, now I want to change gears and specifically address parents with young children, grandchildren, and even older children.

As a parent and or a grandparent, you play a significant role in influencing your child's self-esteem. Your children will eventually take on a life of their own and write their own stories, but in the beginning pages of their life, you, as a parent and or a grandparent, have a great deal of influence as to how that story may go...

The way we talk to our children becomes their inner voice.
– Peggy O'Mara

The life we live and the words we speak into our children can create life and death for their future. I wish I would have discovered the *quick-charge* concept before I ever married or we had our children. I could have infused my children with more of the *quick-charge life* when they were little. I am certain I would have done a better job of building their self-esteem if I had a better mindset many years ago, but it's never too late. I am certain I would have been a more loving and accepting husband as well, but again, I must move aside those boulders and climb my life mountain to see the glorious views ahead.

The good news is I have the *quick-charge* concept firmly engrafted into my life now! I am continually building wonderful memories with my kids and grandkids and climbing my mountain every day to experience new heights! I have made a ton of incredible memories with my children and grandchildren.

I will continue building fishing memories with my son Andrew. Many of our memories are created when we go fishing or share other successes together. Only the other day he was given a prestigious award at work for his past five years of dedicated service! He sent me a text later that day to share the good news and thank me for rearing him to be the man he is today! I know of nothing in this world like the feeling that comes from hearing words of admiration from your child. I am quick these days to infuse my son's life with positive affirmations. I let him know often that I love him and tell him how proud of him I am. I seek to find opportunities to tell both of my kids and grandkids exactly how proud I am of them, and I do my best to support them in their endeavors in life.

My daughter Kristina was quite sick a few years ago, and I sat with her in the hospital for two days as many parents would do. When she got out of the hospital, she posted a beautiful account online of her love and admiration for me as her father. I was very humbled by her expression of gratefulness to have me as an example of a loving father. Again, I know of no words to describe how proud I was of my daughter for being so open and caring toward me.

My kids have now developed lives of their own with families of their own as well. Some of the impact I wish I would have had when they were younger is gone, but I did the best I could with what I knew back then. I guess I did fairly well because they are both wonderful humans, parents, and they express their love and a deep appreciation for me often which is worth more to me than anything.

I am privileged to have a tribe of grandchildren (and another one to be born any day) whom I can influence from a young age. Some of my grandchildren are blood-related and some are not, but I have an important obligation to live and speak the *quick-charge life* concept into all of their lives.

The following are some suggestions to help you build an unshakable self-esteem in your children and grandchildren's lives:

- Pray for them always.
- Listen to their concerns and rejoice in their accomplishments.
- Speak positive words into their lives whenever the opportunities arise.
- Live the *quick-charge life* as an example for them to follow.
- Teach them to live the *quick-charge life!*

The *Quick Charge Concept* is about:

- Developing a personal relationship with the Lord and continually seeking Him to energize you with His power.

- Taking responsibility for your happiness by thinking positive thoughts—no matter what you may encounter in life.
- Learning to be calm and trusting the Lord during the storms in your life.
- Finding joy and blessing when you inspire others.
- Generously giving of all that God has given you.

In a nutshell, the *quick-charge life* is an invitation for you to intentionally, deliberately and consciously change the way you think so that you might discover all the *quick-charge* outlets God surrounds you with every single day of your life. The *quick-charge* concept will allow you to continually charge the power already living within you to move past your perceived limitations and boldly step into the life you were born to create!

Learn it, live it, and inspire others—*Quick Charge Your Life!*

As I was travelling home from work one day, I was listening to an audio book titled *The 7 Habits of Highly Effective People* by Steven R. Covey. I found it interesting that Steven was giving an example about a lesson he learned while trying to teach and discipline one of his daughters about sharing. His illustration reminded me of my own daughter and how she can be incredibly strong-willed at times.

When Kristina was little, I remember how she would always grab her fork or whatever eating utensil she needed at the time and start eating with her left hand. I would quickly switch it to her right hand, but she would soon switch back to using her left, and the routine would continue. We would go through the same routine with pencils and pens as well.

Curiously, one day I had a revelation. I realized that maybe my daughter was actually left-handed. Since everyone else in my immediate family was right-handed, we automatically assumed she was also right-handed. So, when she would try to do things with her left hand, I automatically figured she was confused about which hand to use when eating or drawing, and I would correct her. That she could possibly be left-handed never even occurred to me at first.

I love her so much, and one of the attributes I appreciate about her (besides the fact she is left-handed) is that she is a strong-willed person. She is also an amazing mother, which is one of the many characteristics I am so grateful for with both of my kids. They both possess such a love and dedication to their children.

As I thought about the lesson that Steven was teaching with the illustration about his daughter, I began recounting lessons I had tried to teach my kids when they were little. I then stopped, and as I thought about self-esteem, I could not recall anyone ever teaching me the importance of specifically building self-esteem in my children.

I do remember that my parents always expressed the importance of making certain I told my kids how much I loved and appreciated them, which certainly would help build their self-esteem. I also remember them teaching me about proper discipline and many other aspects of parenting, but I do not recall anyone ever specifically teaching me the importance and role I played as a parent in helping them build an *unshakable self-esteem*.

Parents and grandparents who still have young children in their life, I cannot stress enough your vitally important role in writing the first pages of your child's life story. It is so important that their lives be filled with positive affirmations, love, support, and purpose to help them build an *unshakable self-esteem*.

20 Affirmations to Build Your Child's Self-Esteem
by Cyndi Barber

1. "I love you." (You can never speak your love enough.)
2. "I appreciate you."
3. "I believe in you."
4. "I love how you care about others."
5. "I'm proud of you and of who you are."
6. "My life is better with you in it."
7. "You are enough just as you are."
8. "You are fun to have around."
9. "You are excellent at ____."
10. "You are smart."
11. "You are beautiful/handsome."
12. "You are courageous."
13. "You are wonderfully unique."
14. "You are talented."
15. "You are a good friend."
16. "You have really great ideas."
17. "You are a gift to our family."
18. "You are a great kid. It's a privilege to know you."
19. "You make a positive difference wherever you go."
20. "You have what it takes to be successful in life."

Learn it, live it, and inspire others! *Quick Charge Your Life! Unshakable Self-Esteem*

Parents need to fill a child's bucket of self-esteem so high that the rest of the world can't poke enough holes to drain it dry...

– Alvin Price

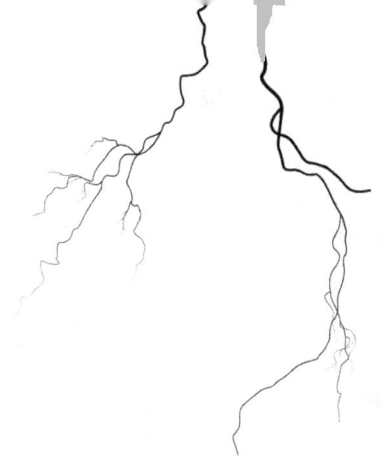

CHAPTER EIGHT

Learn to Love Yourself

In chapter one I referred to the fact that I needed to check my own life to assess how I felt about my personal self-esteem in order. I wanted to determine if I felt qualified to write about the topic of *unshakable self-esteem* to help others. In chapter two I examined what self-esteem really meant or what it is exactly.

When examining my own self-esteem and then researching what self-esteem really is, I felt that the concept of learning to **love yourself** was one of the more crucial aspects of truly building an unshakable self-esteem.

You can love many things. You can love tacos or steak or ____ (fill in the blank with your favorite food). You can love your car. You can love a certain vacation spot. You can love your dog, a cat, or a horse. You can even love others. You can love fishing or golfing or ___. This entire list is composed of things of activities that seem fairly easy to love. However, loving yourself is a much deeper and a more challenging concept to grasp at times.

What does it really mean to love yourself? Once again, a quick online search revealed the following short, concise answer:

To love yourself means to accept yourself as you are and to come to terms with those aspects of yourself that you cannot change. It means to have self-respect, a positive self-image, and unconditional self-acceptance.

Though this answer is good, I feel the concept is perhaps a little too vague to learn how to love yourself. As I continued my research, one of the first thoughts that came to my mind was a saying: you can't love others until you can first love yourself. I even found a quote by Leo Buscaglia to support the idea!

To love others, you must first love yourself.
– Leo Buscaglia

However, that is only a man's quote and not the gospel. Must you love yourself in order to love others? I personally don't believe you must absolutely love yourself in order to love someone else or to love other things. However, I believe the bigger issue is that it really comes down to happiness. If you don't love yourself, then I do not believe you can ever truly be happy. If you cannot be happy, then how can you possibly build an unshakable self-esteem and love yourself? Therefore, it seems vital to me that some serious effort needs to be dedicated to investigate **love** and discover exactly how you can learn to love yourself.

The online answer I found said to accept yourself as you are. I know many people who struggle with that concept and need a better understanding. So, as I have already mentioned, we need to dig deeper. The answer further said to have self-respect, a positive self-image, and unconditional self-acceptance, which are important aspects that have already been addressed in varying degrees.

Perhaps learning to love yourself starts by loving your body since we walk around in our body and see it in the mirror. A poor self-image based on one's physical appearance often leads to many people's developing depression and low self-esteem because they do not like the image staring back at them. However, basing self-love on how you view your body means looking at the many different aspects of the body, i.e., your height, weight, eyes, hair, hands, feet, skin, and the color of your hair, the size of your hands, the condition of your fingernails, etc.

I do not know of many people who absolutely **LOVE** everything about their body or physical appearance. Most people are always trying to improve or change their body's appearance. I believe that using the body as a true measure of how much we love ourselves would be quite difficult.

If you had the perfect body and perfect everything else from a physical standpoint, you might enjoy that aspect of your life, but does that so-called perfection really define whether or not you love yourself? If you are subconscious about your height based on what would seem normal for your gender and age, then that aspect could wear on your self-esteem. Obviously, changing those aspects of yourself would be quite difficult. But if you can learn to accept that you are the height you are or the race that you are or the gender you are, then you can learn to **love** yourself!

I do not believe your physical appearance can accurately determine if you love yourself. Perhaps you would have some satisfaction or self-confidence in yourself if you placed importance on your physical appearance, and that effort is totally acceptable. However, your physical appearance can change due to age, accidents, or illness.

I believe loving yourself demands much more than a physical appearance. I remember my mom always saying, "Tommy, you should love a girl for who she was and not for how she looks." This is about **YOU** now, so you should not accept anything less than to be loved by yourself for who you are—not by how you look!

I do believe we can wish things were different about various aspects of our physical and social status, and we can strive to make the changes to the best of our ability, but we can develop an unshakable self-esteem even if we do not have the perfect body, the perfect smile, or the perfect hair. In fact, you do not even need to be close to perfect at all!

I want to take a closer look at the definition of **LOVE** from dictionary.com to gain a better understanding of the word:

Noun:

- a profoundly tender, passionate affection for another person
- a feeling of warm personal attachment or deep affection, as for a parent, a child, or friend
- sexual passion or desire
- a person toward whom love is felt; beloved person; sweetheart
- (used in direct address as a term of endearment, affection, or the like): *Would you like to see a movie, love?*
- a love affair; an intensely amorous incident; amour
- sexual intercourse; copulation
- [*initial capital letter*] a personification of sexual affection, as Eros or Cupid

Learn to Love Yourself

- affectionate concern for the well-being of others: *the love of one's neighbor*
- strong predilection, enthusiasm, or liking for anything: *her love of books*
- the object or thing so liked: *The theater was her great love*
- the benevolent affection of God for His creatures, or the reverent affection due from them to God
- *Chiefly tennis*: a score of zero; nothing
- a word formerly used in communications to represent the letter *L*.

Verb (*used with object*), *loved, lov·ing*

- to have love or affection for: *All her pupils love her.*
- to have a profoundly tender, passionate affection for (another person).
- to have a strong liking for; take great pleasure in: *to love music.*
- to need or require; benefit greatly from: *Plants love sunlight.*
- to embrace and kiss [someone], as a lover
- to have sexual intercourse with

When I look over this long list of examples and or definitions from the dictionary of what *love* is, I do not read any meaning that definitively explains how people are supposed to love themselves. I can clearly see how we can love another person or express our love toward another person or other things, but nothing really directly relates to how people are supposed to *love* themselves.

I dug deeper and found a much better description of what *love* really is in 1 Corinthians 13:4-7 (NIV):

> *Love is patient, love is kind. It does not envy, it does not boast, it is not proud. [5]It does not dishonor others, it is not self-seeking, it is not easily angered, it keeps no record of wrongs. [6]Love does not delight in evil but rejoices with the truth. [7]It always protects, always trusts, always hopes, always perseveres.*

Examine your life and see if you love yourself based on what Scripture defines as love.

1. **Are you patient with yourself and others?** Do you show patience toward others regardless of the situation? You can become impatient with someone or something at times and correct yourself for your wrongdoing.

   I am reminded of a story told by Steven R. Covey in his book *The 7 Habits of Highly Effective People:*

   A young man and his children entered the subway one day while Steven was traveling. The man sat next to him while the kids continued to run around being very disruptive. They were grabbing other people's newspapers and yelling. The father was just sitting in his seat with his head down, seemingly oblivious to the severity of the situation. Steven recounts how he sat there and thought to himself, *How could this man possibly allow his children to be so disrespectful of others and not even care or reprimand them?* Finally, he decided to bring the incident to the man's attention, suggesting that he attend to his children.

   The man, with a deep sigh, replied, "You are right. I don't know what I was thinking. We just came from the hospital where their mother died an hour ago. I guess I just did not notice. I am sorry.

Of course, you can only imagine how the author felt about his suggestion or how anyone would have felt in that moment.

Change your paradigm! One minute you are getting impatient with how someone is reacting or handling a situation, and the very next minute you have a paradigm shift in your thinking as you realize the person in question has far greater issues on his mind to deal with than you do. So, perhaps you need to shift your own paradigm at times when it comes to being impatient with others or even yourself.

Another question perhaps to ask yourself is: do I recognize the areas that can be changed in my life (e.g., finances, job, weight, lifestyle, etc.), but am I willing to be patient enough with myself as I work on needed changes until they happen?

2. **Are you kind to yourself and others?** You might be kind to some and not to others. Are you consistent in making kindness part of your DNA regardless of the circumstances?

    Do you allow yourself to be okay with making honest mistakes and understanding you can do better and keep trying? Are you kind to yourself by feeding your mind with positive thoughts?

3. **Do you check yourself to make certain you are not envious, boastful, and prideful?** If you are envious of someone else's looks or want to be like that person, then you will not have a good self-image of yourself. If

you are prideful, you will always place more value on yourself over others. Spotting people who have these character flaws is often easy.

4. **Do you dishonor yourself or others?** How do you view and/or treat others? How do you treat yourself? If you abuse your body with drugs and or alcohol, you are not honoring the temple that God has given to you.

5. **Are you self-seeking?** Where is the light or focus shining? If the focus is on you, then you have the wrong focus. Man was created to serve and honor others.

6. **Do you get angry with others and or at yourself?** Can you accept your faults and weaknesses in order to work on the things you are able? I believe that humble people who are slow to anger will project the same attitude of forgiveness and acceptance toward others.

7. **Are you quick to forgive yourself and forgive others?** Forgiveness is a difficult concept to judge in another because it is often based on yourself or someone else's level of wrongdoing. You might quickly forgive someone for things that did not cost you much but dislike someone who cost you dearly. The same might be true for yourself. You might beat yourself up over bad choices or lost opportunities, but you must be willing to forgive yourself. A level of wrongdoing should not be a measurement. Some people can forgive another when the person might have murdered one of their loved ones. On the other hand, that same offense would be almost unforgivable for someone else.

Are you able to forgive yourself for mistakes that have been very costly in your life? You can develop a low self-esteem if you allow guilt and shame to fester inside of you over things you have done or over things others have done that you are unwilling to forgive.

8. **Do you shun things that are evil, and rejoice in the good?** This point can also be debated. What is considered evil, and what is considered good? Some things are obviously evil, and some things are definitely good, but in general, do you hope the best for others and not purpose to promote anything that is evil and unjust?

9. **Do you protect yourself and others?** You should be mindful to protect yourself and those close to you from any bad influences.

10. **Do you guard your mind from negative things?** So much negativity exists all around us in the world today. You must guard your mind and fill it with positive affirmations.

11. **Do you trust yourself?** Do you make good choices as to what you do and with whom you associate? Are you able to resist temptation when you are with friends?

12. **Do you have hope?** Love is always hopeful and seeks the best in all things.

13. **Do you persevere?** Love will always commit to staying the course until you reach your goals. In marriage we vow "for better, for worse, for richer, for poorer, in

sickness and in health, until death do us part." You can learn to love yourself the same way...

I could write an entire book on this one subject alone! As you continue to read 1 Corinthians 13:4-7 repeatedly, follow and utilize this wonderful road map in learning to love yourself and others. You will build unshakable self-esteem!

I believe my mother had great hopes for me, but she always said that she hoped I would be a loving person above all. Being a loving person goes well beyond simply saying the three little words, "**I love you**" or even declaring, "**I love myself**." You must continually check and ask yourself if you are living out 1 Corinthians 13:4-7.

Learn it, live it, and inspire others! *Quick Charge Your Life! Unshakable Self-Esteem*

One of the greatest regrets in life is being what others would want you to be, rather than being yourself.

—Shannon L. Alder

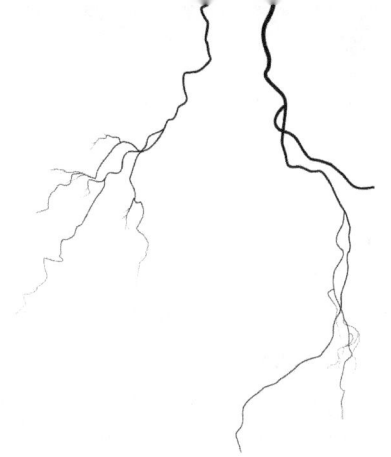

CHAPTER NINE

Throw Out the Lemonade

The previous chapter addressed the subject of loving yourself. Love, which is exquisitely detailed and delicate, cuts to the core of who you really are. Love also exposes you and opens you up so you can build an unshakable self-esteem. The willingness to expose your life and opening up to love makes you vulnerable. Love can bring incredible joy, while also carrying the risk of causing great pain. In that vulnerability and risk of pain, greatness is born.

The entire process of facing your failures, hurts, shortcomings, disappointments, and unanswered questions about your life can best be described as "open-heart surgery." However, unlike a normal surgery, you can often feel the pain in life cutting and slicing on you, even allowing you to see the major surgery being performed. Some deeply sensitive and possibly very painful areas of your life may have been exposed thus far in the book. Perhaps the details shared about abuse, torment, and bullying have filleted anew some severe pain and embarrassment in your life. Maybe you have had to face your deformities, illnesses or other physical issues head on as accepting yourself and persevering were addressed. Maybe you know you want to move beyond your pain and unfair situations that make your life difficult to navigate and have held you back from achieving your dreams and goals, but you still feel lost and hopeless.

Chances are you have been made aware of faults, weakness, and issues that you try so hard to keep hidden and buried inside, but you must expose them and allow yourself to become vulnerable. Maybe you don't even know why you are the way you are. Perhaps you're shy or can't seem to speak up or get to the top. Perhaps you try to be happy, but it just never seems to go your way.

Whatever the case may be, if you truly want to build an unshakable self-esteem and rise to the top of your life's mountain, you must be open, allowing all the pain, disappointments, troubles, insecurities, and shame to be exposed. Once the surgery of life's struggles and pain has opened you up, only then can you begin to heal.

Now is the time to test and see if the first surgery was successful. Yes, I said *first* surgery! This chapter will get to the bottom line, cut deeper and really address the issue of what it takes to have confidence in your ability to build an unshakable self-esteem. My friend, do you have what it takes to believe in yourself and see yourself as someone who can get whatever it is YOU want out of life?

What would you do in life if you possessed an unshakable self-esteem? Why not list some goals and dreams on a piece of paper or even in this book? I mean, what if you knew nothing mattered other than what you say mattered? What if you no longer allowed yourself to be subjected to the opinions of others?

Imagine for a moment that YOU no longer have the need to seek approval from a spouse, a friend, or a parent. What if you awakened from this "surgery," and you had an unshakable confidence in yourself to do whatever you want, regardless of the size of the dream or vision? What if you awakened tomorrow morning, and you somehow know that regardless of whatever life throws at you, YOU are going to climb to the top of your mountain in life and ROAR? What if you finally realized that what you really want is simply to **LIKE** yourself enough to move past your perceived limitations and boldly step into the life you were born to create?

Yes, after all the surgery is over and you have exposed everything that holds you back, the bottom-line motivator is simply to **like** yourself. You are finally ready to discover how to truly like yourself. Please let this possibility sink in for a minute.

For most people, life will bring you some lemons along the way. So, what do you do with lemons? You have likely heard that proverbial phrase used to encourage others: if life gives you lemons, _____ _____!

Sorry, I purposely did not fill in the blanks because I am NOT going to make lemonade. The problem with simply making lemonade is that it never gives you the visual and mental power that resides within you to really face the big stuff in life. If you are battling a low self-image because of something that has caused you great pain and trauma in life, then trying to sugarcoat it and tossing lemons in a pitcher of water to make lemonade is just not enough! Please visualize the following exercise with me.

Think Lemon!

Imagine a real lemon, see yourself picking up that lemon, and feeling both the rough and smooth textures of the rind in your hand. Now imagine barely squeezing the lemon in your hand—just enough to visualize squeezing it and feeling its shape in your hand. Now imagine holding up the lemon at eye level and examining its bright-yellow peel.

See yourself scraping a little bit of the rind or peeling back a portion with your fingernail. Hold that lemon up to your nose to smell its clean, fresh, and potent odor. Imagine how bitter that lemon would taste if you were to bite into it. Allow the saliva in your mouth to water.

Imagine **biting** off a chunk and begin chewing it. Feel that lemon swishing its juice around in your mouth and then as it trickles down your throat. Take another bite, chew up the pulp, suck on the sour juice, and devour that entire lemon regardless of the sour taste! Although that fruit may be bitter and make you almost drool, you can eat that lemon!

"Why" you may ask, "would you eat a lemon?" Because I can assure you that life will give you lemons at times. Remember this exercise of eating lemons as a metaphor for the issues that will come to your life. I believe applying this metaphor will help you as the pains and frustrations of life come at you.

Be careful not to always anticipate lemons in life. Life will give you sweet things as well, but handling the good stuff of life is easy! You will attract good and sweet things into your life when you have an unshakable self-esteem! But life will always present some challenges or "lemons" that will test your self-esteem, self-confidence, self-image, self-worth, self-identity, self-love, and anything else you might call on to find out who you are in life.

However, when life gives you lemons, do not avoid those lemons by trying to cut them up and tossing them into some juice pitcher with sugar to make them sweeter. Be **UNSHAKABLE!** Grab that lemon and bite into it! Chew it up and show those lemons in life that you are not ashamed or afraid of who you are.

We need to return to surgery one last time... Count backward starting from 99, 98, 97, 96, 9....

- Maybe your parents got divorced when you were little, and you did not get the life you wished you could have or should have had.
- Maybe you were born with less-than-favorable genes, and you fight your weight, your complexion, your hair or face a myriad of other physical issues.
- Maybe you were born with a deformity or other disability that makes life more difficult and challenging.
- Maybe you have deficiency that makes you feel stupid or less acceptable than others, so you have avoided reaching for your dreams to save embarrassment and failure.
- Maybe you were violated, molested, beaten, and have scars so deep you are certain nobody will ever understand or love you.
- Perhaps you have made horrible mistakes in life that have cost you dearly, and now you feel buried by your troubles and feel you will never find a way out.
- Maybe you have been in a car accident or other type of accident that left you paralyzed, disabled, or mentally and physically scarred in some way.
- Maybe you feel you are too short or too tall.

- Maybe you lost a parent at a young age, or you were abandoned by your parents and have been placed in multiple foster homes.
- Maybe your father walked out of your life at a young age, and you have no relationship or only a broken relationship and wonder why he does not love you.
- Maybe you have lost all your money or have faced so much loss in your life that you no longer believe you deserve a fair shot at a good job.
- Maybe your spouse cheated on you, and you have been left to fend for life on your own.
- Maybe you are the one who cheated, and now you're miserable and riddled with guilt and shame.
- Maybe you have PTSD nightmares from serving in the military that come on unexpectedly, and you are scared to do anything for fear of the visions returning.
- Maybe you have secrets so dark you have convinced yourself that you do not deserve to be happy or to live a life of freedom.
- Maybe you have been continually yelled at, threatened, and abused verbally and/or physically to the point that you are so broken and beaten you don't care anymore.
- Maybe one of your children died or you miscarried or had an abortion, or your child is missing with unanswered questions.
- Maybe you wish you were of a different race or culture but have no choice.

Go ahead, feel the very real pain for all of the reason why you may feel broken and unworthy of love. There is no denying that you may have had many wrongs, mistakes, and disappointments in life. Your "surgery" has now ended, and you are waking up!

My friend, your only limitations will be the ones you place on yourself!

All that pain and anger that might have been brought on by any wrongs or bad decisions or loss in your life are your "lemons." Take each lemon one by one, bite into it, and start chewing on it. As you visualize the "lemon's" fullest details that your mind will allow, feel that lemon in your mouth and taste its juices. That lemon has absolutely nothing on you. You can bite into it and chew it up!

Nothing can stop you from believing in yourself and liking who you are. You have full control over your mind and your beliefs. People can try to break you with their words and actions. Circumstance and bad choices can try to break you, but the only way you can ever be broken is allowing yourself to be broken. You have the power to become unbroken and climb to the top of your life's mountain and **ROAR** in victory!

If you feel like you are dead inside, broken, confused, and hopeless, you are in a good place to start your climb to victory! The good news is that Jesus brings dead things back to life! You're not alone. If you will seek the Lord first, He will give you the strength to climb to the top of your mountain. When you have the Lord by your side, you are never climbing alone!

The Lord is on my side; I will not fear. What can man do to me? ⁷The Lord is on my side as my helper; I shall look in triumph on those who hate me.
— Psalm 118:6-7 (ESV)

> *So do not fear, for I am with you; do not be dismayed, for I am your God. I will strengthen you and help you; I will uphold you with my righteous right hand.*
> — Isaiah 41:10 (NIV)

When God created you, He gave you an incredible mind that is one of the most powerful and valuable assets you have. When you think on positive thoughts and create a vision of what you really want in life, then you can accomplish it!

Now for another exercise: say to yourself, "I like myself!" You read it correctly. Simply say, "I like myself." Keep saying "I like myself," and keep feeding your mind with positive thoughts regardless of whatever negative feelings you may perceive inside until you program your mind to manifest positive images of who you are. By doing so, you are building unshakable self-esteem. You can **LIKE** yourself!

Yes, the bottom line is that everyone really just wants to be able to **like** themselves!

So, throw out the lemonade and learn to bite into the lemons that come your way in life. Realize that you have the ability to bite into ALL the lemons that come your way. You can and will build unshakable self-esteem.

Learn it, live it, and inspire others! *Quick Charge Your Life! Unshakable Self-Esteem*

> *The worst loneliness is not to be comfortable with yourself.*
> – Mark Twain

CHAPTER TEN

What's Your Story?

The last couple of chapters have been designed to cut to the core to expose any possible hidden or known pain you might be carrying from past or current events in your life that weigh on your feeling of self-esteem. I do hope you realize you are not alone and that you can speak new life into your circumstances. There is no pain in your life too great that it cannot be overcome.

One of the most powerful disciplines that I have ever adapted into my own personal life to build an unshakable self-esteem was to start journaling. If done correctly, writing your thoughts and starting a daily journal is a very powerful way to *quick charge your life* and build your self-esteem.

When I began journaling in 2017, I found the practice of learning to record my thoughts and feelings was more of a slow process. In fact, I needed a couple of years to really see the power of journaling in my life. Toward the end of May of 2018, I began to sense a change in my life and in how I saw myself. I had felt like a victim for so many years, but through journaling, I finally began to realize that I had been speaking an incredible amount of negativity into my life. However, even more important than realizing I spoke negativity into my life was the realization that I could speak positive affirmations into my life just as easily. In other words, I realized that I could visualize the life I wanted to live.

We cannot always control what will happen to us in life, but we can control how we process what happens to us and comes our way in life. My dramatic life change was a direct response to all of the research and disciplines I had been applying to my life that led to the discovery of the *quick-charge life* I live today! Through journaling I discovered my strong passion for writing and researching, and thus, launched me into a whole new phase of life as an author.

I am not mentioning journaling alone as a nice idea to consider. I am **strongly suggesting** that you also adopt the daily practice of journaling in your own life daily! I have found that recording your thoughts through journaling really is one of the most powerful keys to living a life of success that you can practice and is one of the key components to the *quick-charge* concept. Journaling and recording positive affirmations for your life will help you take your self-esteem to a whole new level. Putting your thoughts into written words will help give you a visual of what is going on inside your head.

The *quick-charge* moment is when you turn any negative thoughts around and into a record of positive affirmations and begin speaking those positive words into your life. All my life I have heard the idiom, "Seeing is believing," and reading (seeing) positive words in a journal will help a person believe what he has written.

My journal notes are focused on the positives of my life as I have been employing the *quick-charge* concept for some

What's Your Story?

time now. My journal is a series of positive affirmations that I record to speak into my life and to encourage or remind myself that each day was a great day! On the good days, I do not need to change anything as I am uplifted and *quick charged* as I record my day's events and thoughts in my journal. However, I do have days when I struggle, my energy is low, and I need a boost. Even as I pen this chapter, I had one of those difficult thought days, and thus this new chapter was born.

I want to share a short personal entry from my journal that I wrote several months ago. To give you some perspective, I was writing this account early on in the writing process for my first book, *Quick Charge Your Life*.

> I'm struggling today with some doubt. Am I crazy for putting so much time and money into this *quick-charge* project that I literally thought of only a few days ago? Although today has been a productive day, I am tired and wonder if I am dreaming too big?
>
> I penned some good thoughts today so I'm off and running on this project, but I do have my doubts. Maybe I should slow down and not waste my money since I really have no experience as an author.

— The *Quick-Charge* Moment —

As I read these journal notes back to myself, I realized I needed to put aside any negative thoughts and doubts and speak only positive affirmations to myself. I quickly went to work writing and added a new, updated journal entry.

> I refuse to allow myself to stop! I will be successful, and although I am yet to become a seasoned author or to get this book published, I can produce a book that will change lives. If my efforts help only one person to propel himself to a *quick-charge life* as he reads this book, I will do it. If my endeavor helps thousands or even millions find a newfound energy to propel them to great success, I will do it. The fact is, I will be successful by simply getting this book into print. I can do it...I will do it...I will *quick charge my life* every single day until I successfully publish this book...I need not know how or when.
>
> Wow, I am super-charged right now! The energy flowing through my body after that quick charge is palpable! It's hard to believe I was so down and drained of energy just a minute ago prior to writing this journal entry...

How I hope you are grasping exactly how powerful it is to *Quick Charge Your Life* by quickly replacing any negative, toxic thoughts or negative talk with positive affirmations and belief in yourself! Regardless of the situation you're in right now, I can tell you that God made you to become someone incredible. Perhaps you do not believe you can do anything with your life now or that somehow you missed out. If so, I can assure you if you will simply start *quick charging your life* daily, you can and will change your self-esteem and embrace incredible new levels of success.

The person who taps into the *quick-charge life* knows no failure. God does not make mistakes. If you simply do not allow any negative thoughts to stay inside your head, you can power through anything. No matter what level of success a person reaches, he will have doubts at times or feel tired and drained. It's life; however, we have the incredible God-given ability to *quick charge* our lives by replacing that negative energy and infusing it with positive thoughts.

So, if you're not already journaling, why not get started on a journaling plan now?

I use my laptop most of the time to journal. The times when I am not near my laptop or on the nights I forget to journal, I often remember as I start to rest my head on the pillow. My eyes will open, and I will suddenly remember that I need to make a journal entry for the day. I am such a firm believer in the power of tracking my thoughts by journaling that I try not to miss a day if I can possibly avoid it. On those days when I might let it slip and remember at the last minute as I am going to bed, I grab my iPhone and make some journal entries in the notes section. Then I can sleep. The next day, I copy them to my laptop journal notes. Admittedly, life does get busy at times, and I record a few days of journal notes on my iPhone notes before I copy them to my laptop.

I have found that following these few rules makes journaling purposeful.

1. Write what is really on your mind.
2. After creating a journal entry go back and re-read your entry. Purpose to change any negative thoughts.

Re-write a new journal entry below the first entry, flipping your negative thoughts into positive ones.
3. Try to discipline yourself to journal every single day.
4. Take the time to look back over your past history of journal notes from time to time to track your progress.

Understand that journaling and creating positive daily thought habits to build your self-esteem are no different than starting a workout plan to improve your health. You **MUST** stay disciplined and consistently write entries until journaling becomes a habit.

Allow yourself to feel a *quick charge* as you recount your successes you have recorded in your journal notes.

There are no rules as to how long or how short your daily journal entries need to be. Some days I only have a few thoughts, and other days I write a page or two of thoughts. Write as much or as little as you feel like writing each day but be certain to make the effort to journal every day.

May I caution you that to expect days when you might have to talk yourself into journaling and work really hard to make the thoughts positive. At other times when you simply do not feel like being positive as the daily burdens may weigh too heavy, I can assure you that on those days in particular you will have the greatest opportunity to grow. Those days will help you reach new levels in your growth as you climb your mountain and build a positive mindset. Again, journaling is no different than working out. You must fight through the "burn" and keep pressing forward with positive affirmations.

Just like with the journaling process when I am working on writing a book, I purpose to write for a while, and I desperately try not to go back and read what I have written or do any editing until after I have finished my thought process for a chapter or a section within a chapter. You must practice the same discipline when you journal. Simply write your thoughts the way they come to you without any sugarcoating or trying to make them all positive and nice. I have days when I am so *quick-charged*, writing a very positive account of my day is easy. It happens often now, but I have days when I am going through tough stuff too.

Once I get on a roll, I like to keep on keeping on with my typing. I will often make a ton of silly spelling mistakes and other errors. In fact, you might be amazed at how scattered my thoughts are and how many spelling errors I make when I get to typing with a fury... Good grief, the errors I found after I finished with the writing flurry for this section of my book was very comical. I often laugh at myself when I go back and re-read some of what I type. But I have found it's the best way for me to keep flowing with a thought. Recording your thoughts and going until you're finished will be the best way for you to journal your thoughts too.

Once you finish with a writing flurry that captures your spur-of-the-moment thoughts on the computer, then and **only** then should you go back and read through that journal entry. Feel free to make corrections in spelling, grammar, and infuse it with positive affirmations.

So, I shared **ALL** of that to say when you go back to reread your thoughts, **DO NOT** erase your original thoughts. Yes, make spelling and grammatical corrections, but DO NOT edit the original thought. This step is important! You simply want to find a better or more positive way to express your thoughts following the original thought as a new positive journal entry—if need be. By keeping the original thoughts, you will be able to see the change. You will see your progress and get an idea for how it feels to turn it around into a positive thought. Hopefully, you will experience *quick-charge* moments as you create a new positive thought.

I promise, if you will dedicate 30 to 60 days to making journaling a habit and stay consistent to infuse positive thoughts into EVERY entry, you will be *quick charged!* In time, your self-esteem will grow until you see yourself in a whole new perspective!

Learn it, live it, and inspire others! *Quick Charge Your Life! Unshakable Self-Esteem*

The better you feel about yourself, the less you feel the need to show off.

– Robert Hand

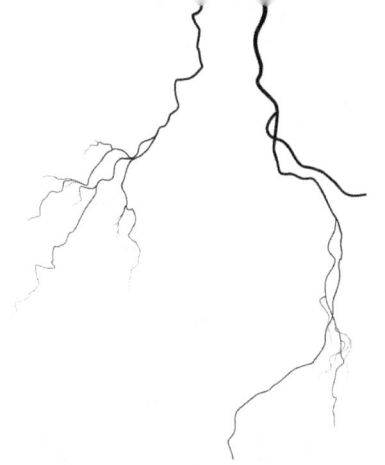

CHAPTER ELEVEN

The Chicken or the Egg?

I feel sure you have probably pondered the question or heard debates by many as to whether the chicken or the egg came first. Unfortunately, I cannot solve that problematic question in this chapter, but thinking about this question made me consider what came first for humans when it comes to self-esteem.

Are we born with a pre-determined level of self-esteem? Perhaps we are more inclined to first have a poor or maybe even a neutral self-esteem when we are born. These questions generated a curiosity of whether or not someone is more easily inclined to develop a low self-esteem over a healthy self-esteem.

In order to develop a healthy self-esteem, seemingly you would need to purpose to work at it. However, you must also work at developing a low self-esteem as well. Think about it. You must make decisions everyday as to what you believe about yourself. Both good and bad images of yourself take thought and work, but the fact remains that you alone choose to like yourself.

Obviously, each person is subjected to different circumstances on a daily basis. At the end of the day, only you can make the choice of whether or not you like yourself.

Perhaps you might be thinking about someone who is subjected to terrible abuse and treated poorly. Surely victims of abuse are more inclined to develop a low self-esteem versus someone who lives in a healthy environment of encouragement and is fed positive affirmations. Yes, I agree; liking yourself in a positive environment would seemingly be much easier, but still, I would argue that at the end of the day you must make the choice to like yourself—whether or not it's easier for some.

I was listening to an online sermon by Steven Furtick, and he made the following statement at the beginning of his sermon: *you always become what you believe.* That statement gave me a *quick-charge* moment that I could file away to contemplate when I needed a boost in the future, not to mention the boost it gave me at that moment.

Perhaps a neutral self-esteem is where we first begin in life since an infant or a toddler would not yet know how to properly build his own self-esteem to form a valid opinion of himself. I do believe many kids do consciously begin to form opinions of themselves at a young age.

In conducting some research, I found articles arguing both sides of the genes debate. Some purported that self-esteem is created as we grow and live our lives. Others say that research is still being done on finding certain genes within us that might determine our self-esteem makeup.

At the beginning of this book, I asked myself if I felt qualified to write on the topic of self-esteem. After all, many of the books and articles I studied myself as I gathered information and ideas for this topic were written by people with earned PHDs and MDs. My only degree is what I call a life-experience

The Chicken or the Egg?

degree. I am not a doctor, a counselor, a psychologist or any authority figure who can make any claims as to my scientific research or discoveries. I have great respect and appreciation for those who have earned their degrees and credentials to help us gain a much greater understanding of how various genes and chromosomes shape who we are.

I feel confident that no one book or study on this topic or any other topic I might address in future books in my *Quick Charge Your Life* series will give you ALL the answers you may need. The one book I will say that has all the key answers to life is the Bible, but I do believe God created many people like myself with the strong desire to record their thoughts and ideas in order to publish books on topics of their expertise, or in my case, personal experience and interest.

My non-medical, non-degree two cents worth when it comes to the debate of whether or not we are born with a set gene that determines our self-esteem is as follows: I cannot say for sure if we have genes that make us more prone to having a healthy or a low self-esteem. However, I am confident in my own personal opinion that unshakable self-esteem is something we must build.

I was watching a video the other day featuring an interview with Bill Gates and Warren Buffett. When the interviewer asked Mr. Buffett why he thought he had taken an interest in investing at the age of six or seven, the billionaire replied, "I guess because I was too dumb to learn about it when I was four."

Although Buffett's response was clever, it did make me wonder at what age people who have built an unshakable self-esteem start taking an interest in how they viewed themselves.

I will assume that the average age of those reading this book will range between 40 to 70 years old. Obviously, some will be younger or older, but I doubt many teenagers or younger kids will be reading this book. One of my passions is inspiring people.

I strongly feel that inspiring children to take an interest in who they are when they are young and teaching them the importance of developing an unshakable self-esteem is imperative.

Whether or not we can agree that all are born with a certain gene that determines our self-esteem, I believe we can agree to disagree on this subject. The one argument that I did find in various articles and books about this particular idea was that regardless of whether or not someone actually has genes that might determine his self-esteem at birth, many researchers readily agreed that the environment into which a person is born can greatly determine the health of a person's self-esteem.

I do agree that an individual's self-esteem may be influenced by the circumstances or environments into which they're born or live can set them on a course. I DO NOT feel that the direction they are headed determines their **final destination**. True, people can develop opinions of themselves—both good or bad—based on whether or not they were born into a loving home versus an abusive home or a supportive environment versus a non-supportive environment. But two people can start life in the same environment and be thrust in the same direction and end up at totally different destinations.

What a person is exposed to can greatly shape how he will develop as a child and into his adulthood, but HE still writes the book and ending. An endless list could be compiled of all the influences that may shape a person's self-esteem. I still contend that regardless of a person's circumstances, he can still control his own opinion of himself.

I am reminded of identical twins who grew up with an alcoholic father. One twin became quite successful, and the other became an alcoholic like his father. When both sons were asked why they felt they had developed the lives they did, the successful son said, "I had to be successful because I refused

The Chicken or the Egg?

to believe I was going to be like my dad." The other son replied, "I had no choice. My dad was an alcoholic, so it was the only life I knew." Both were subjected to the same environment, yet the twins chose radically different paths.

If work is required to develop your self-esteem whether it be high or low, then which is easier to develop? If you had asked me that question a few years ago, I would have likely said that the only one that takes real work to build is unshakable self-esteem. After all, life is what it is, and some people simply do not catch the breaks that others do.

You can blame your parents, your spouse, your siblings, your boss, the environment in which you were reared or whatever else for the views you have of yourself. Allow all that blame to accumulate in your mind, and you can say, "It's just too hard to stay positive and believe in myself."

I have a totally different viewpoint now. Once I discovered and applied the *quick-charge* concept to living my life, I learned that believing in myself and liking myself was actually easier than staying miserable! Things do not always go right in life, but that's life. I find it much easier to feel good about myself and work at viewing life as amazing. I can bite into the lemon or see obstacles like a boulder blocking my path and move them aside as I climb my mountain!

Certainly, I am not perfect and I find myself getting off track or responding negatively toward others at times, but I *quick charge* and get back on track. When I get sick at times and my body feels horrible for a few days, I do not find it so easy to like myself then, but an illness passes. When I have business deals that don't go my way or people disappoint me, it hurts. However, I find *quick charging* easier than spending my energy raging over all the issues and reasons why a project went bad or could go wrong.

Quick Charge Your Life: Unshakable Self-Esteem

You could spend all your energy and time being just as negative about a situation as you can being positive. Remember, "when life gives you lemons, you ____." Yes, you just bite into it and chew! *Quick charge!*

When you see the issues of life piling on top of you, change your view and see them as boulders you can move aside. Keep climbing up your mountain to victory! I have personally had to move many obstacles and eat many lemons in my life that has been filled with many mistakes, heartaches, pains, and disappointments. I have learned to climb and *Quick Charge My Life.* I can choose to like myself because I know I am choosing to climb to the top of my life's mountain rather than be buried by my troubles.

Choose to see your mountain rather than your pile. Choose to climb rather than bury yourself. It's your choice. So, why not choose to like yourself? What about everyone else who still finds it too hard? How can you possibly find the courage to like yourself in the midst of all you face in life or all the failures you've had? Fair enough, in the next chapter I will share some quick and simple steps to help you like yourself and build an unshakable self-esteem!

Learn it, live it, and inspire others! *Quick Charge Your Life! Unshakable Self-Esteem*

I've missed more than 9000 shots in my career. I've lost almost 300 games. Twenty-six times I've been trusted to take the game winning shot and missed. I've failed over and over and over again in my life. And that is why I succeed.

– MICHAEL JORDAN

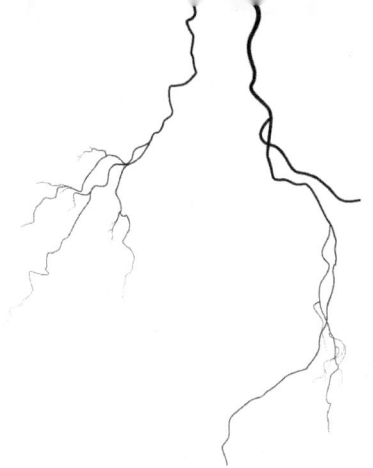

CHAPTER TWELVE

You Asked for It

I still remember the days when I searched for answers as to who, what, where, and why I was placed on this earth. I have always loved being a dad and later a papa. I have loved my career as well. Although I could easily recognize that I had a blessed life, I still struggled with my self-esteem.

I noticed that I especially struggled when people praised me for being a good dad or a person. I never really felt deserving of the praise I received. I carried so much guilt, fear, and shame inside for the many years of bad decisions, tough breaks, and negative self-sabotage in my life. Then, one day I found the truth, though I never really lost it. I guess I should say, I re-discovered I had **it** within me all along.

What was **IT**?

I figured out that I had the ability to change my mind and thought process about myself, and for that matter, about anything and everything I faced in life. Yes, I finally realized that although I may not be able to go back and change my mistakes from my past. I could immediately change the way I viewed my current circumstances and speak positive affirmations into my life and set goals to make a change for my future.

As I promised at the end of the last chapter, I want to share some quick steps you can start using right now to build unshakable self-esteem.

Step One – Change Your View

If you feel lost, hopeless, hurt, and confused about life, then change your view. Study your life's mountain and simply move aside any obstacles blocking you. Fill your life with positive affirmations!

Step Two – Choose to Like Yourself Today!

When you choose to like yourself today and every other day, you will become what you believe! Don't complicate the process. You will become a person who genuinely likes who YOU are!

Step Three – Write Down Your Goals and Journal!

The goals may take you some time to think over, but you need to clearly define some goals you want to accomplish in life and write them down. Then start a journal and record your progress!

Step Four – Pray, Pray, and Pray Some More, and Believe!

I know praying sounds too simple, but it is powerful. Ask the Lord to give you wisdom and strength to become all that He created you to become and believe He will!

Step Five – Keep Filling the Tank and *Quick Charge!*

Always remember to *quick charge!* See your life's mountain and move aside any obstacles blocking you. Keep filling your life with positive affirmations. Keep telling yourself you like yourself every single day. Keep your goals close and start to journal. Pray, pray, and pray some more, believing. Keep filling the tank and *quick charge*!

I know thick manuals, detailed books, and many other sources are available for building self-esteem. I am certain you can glean even more information from many other good sources with helpful information. However, I do not believe any manual or book will be as powerful as what you record in your own mind!

In the piano business, we have a saying: "There is a piano for every person and a person for every piano." I feel sure this saying holds true for books and information as well. I don't know who will take this information I have shared in five steps and choose to follow them, but I know implementing these steps will work for those who choose to allow them to work.

I love the nuggets and words of wisdom and positive information that I discover as I research, study, and file away *quick-charge* moments each and every day. I would like to share a few good nuggets of wisdom I discovered while researching a book authored by Jim Rohn:

1. Learn how to handle the winter. Wintertime is troubles and difficulty.
2. Learn how to take advantage of the spring; it always follows winter. Spring is opportunity!
3. Learn how to protect your crops all summer. Insects will destroy a crop. All good will be attacked, and all values must be defended.
4. Learn how to reap in the fall without complaining and without apology.

Jim Rohn once told a story that I found to be true in my own life, and I suspect many will be able to relate as well. He shared how he once made a list of all the problems and excuses he had for not succeeding. A wise teacher then looked over the list and said, "I only see one problem. **YOU** are not on it."

It's not what happens that determines the quality and quantity of your life, but rather it's what you do that changes everything!

– JIM ROHN

We are often our own worst enemy, and I am often my own worst enemy. One of my first success mentors, Dayle Maloney, used to say, *"You change your life when you change your mind."*

I tell myself every single day that I will be a success. I take dedicated time to study and research to find nuggets like I have shared in this chapter and throughout my books. I tell myself, "I like myself." Doing so seemed somewhat odd at first, but I am thrilled that I finally found the courage to start putting more effort into making more of my life rather than working so hard to find all the reasons why I couldn't succeed. I had a ton of excuses for why I never seemed to catch a break. I would constantly beat myself up for mistakes I had made in the past. Then I finally took all of the negativity and threw it aside so I could continue to climb my life's mountain. You can choose to do the same. It's your choice, and no one else's!

Learn it, live it, and inspire others! *Quick Charge Your Life! Unshakable Self-Esteem*

Be more concerned with your character than your reputation because your character is what you really are, while your reputation is merely what others think you are.

– JOHN WOODEN

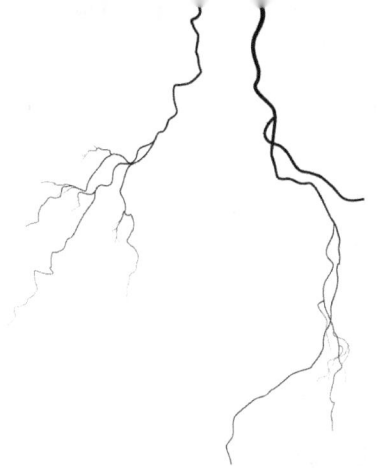

CHAPTER THIRTEEN

Looking Back; Moving Forward

In the first couple of chapters, I introduced the process of choosing and learning about a topic and how I ultimately chose self-esteem. The meaning of self-esteem and how it compared to topics like self-confidence, self-image, and other similar or closely related topics was addressed.

In the next three chapters, I dove into "the deep end of the pool" and addressed some difficult and sensitive topics, including living with any type of disability, illness, and or other imperfections that might make some people feel less than worthy or unable to live a normal life. Chapter three contains a wonderful illustration about a rose representing your life, and even when your life loses petals, it is still a beautiful rose.

Additional sensitive topics are addressed in chapters four and five which presumably opened up some potentially deep wounds and exposed pain for those who have suffered from sexual abuse, verbal abuse, physical abuse, bullying, and other types of unspeakable and horrifying trauma. A mountain concept of moving aside any obstacles that block your path as you climb your mountain to victory was introduced. Adapting this powerful mountain concept paradigm will help you realize no matter how difficult or unfair life has been or may get, you can move aside the obstacles to continue climbing your life's mountain and rise above anything that life has thrown your way—past, present and future.

Both the bad things and the good, positive things in life will also help you climb your life's mountain. You can use anything and everything in your life to climb your mountain. For instance, the *quick-charge* concept that I live is a powerful approach that will allow you to gain strength and help you as you continue to climb your mountain. What is beautiful about climbing the mountain is that once you see yourself starting to climb, you can start to feel good about yourself!

As you climb, you are acting and doing something positive in your life. Even if it's just a few small baby steps each day, you can quickly begin to see better views of yourself and of the life God has designed for you to live. Every step will take you a little higher up the mountain of life, and the views and scenery continue to get better and better!

Chapter six examined another type of low self-esteem that brings on a false sense of security or identity for many. Some people will go from trying to overcompensate for their shortcomings and insecurities and become prideful. Chapter seven focused on the influence and responsibilities we have as parents and grandparents to instill positive self-esteem in our children and grandchildren.

Chapters eight and nine introduced the heart of the matter of people loving themselves. The Scripture, 1 Corinthians 13:4-7, is a wonderful guide to understanding love and having a better understanding of how you can love others and yourself. Chapter nine analyzes the bottom-line motivator of people simply learning to **like** themselves. The powerful illustration

Looking Back; Moving Forward

of throwing out the lemonade and learning to bite into the lemons that life throws your way teaches this motivation.

As I was writing this recap, I thought about the images and paradigm shifts that I have used in my life that I have introduced in this book. I have illustrated the power of biting into the lemons that life throws your way and using all that life piles up in front of you to change your view and see them simply as obstacles that can be moved aside as you climb your mountain to victory instead of burying your dreams and goals.

The reason you need to implement different images is because different situations in life require different perspectives. In the short term, when life gives you a lemon, you can bite into it and quickly bring the moment to a standstill. Maybe a friend disappoints you or you make a mistake or your work day is difficult. Take action and bite into that lemon and deal with it quickly. You can gain confidence and build your self-esteem, knowing you have tools to deal with those situations in your life quickly.

If you are facing an abusive situation or you are caught in a difficult life circumstance that seems out of control, you can choose to visualize those circumstances as boulders that can be moved aside on your journey up your life's mountain. You can see yourself climbing to victory regardless of what you currently face.

In moments of adversity, you can visualize biting into the lemon to quickly dissolve frustration or pain. When you have time to reflect on life, you can build your self-esteem and choose to see the views getting better and better as you climb higher up your life's mountain. You can use the *quick-charge* concept to keep you energized and moving forward to gain the strength to climb higher and experience all that God has created you for. You can see the rose as a beautiful representation of your life—even when it may be missing many petals.

In chapter ten I introduced the wonderful concept of journaling. I **highly** recommend your keeping a journal as a regular practice in your life. You can see how far you have come, which allows you to make needed adjustments to make certain you are moving forward. Chapter eleven examined where and when self-esteem begins in a person's life. Your environment can certainly influence the **direction** of your self-esteem, but it does not have to determine the **final destination**. I further emphasized that regardless of where you were born or how life has treated you, good or bad, at the end of the day you are still in charge of what you think about yourself. You can choose whether or not to **like** yourself.

Chapter twelve includes a quick and simple five-step process to begin building unshakable self-esteem: 1) Change your view, 2) Choose to like yourself today, 3) Write down your goals and journal, 4) Pray and believe, 5) Keep filling the tank and *quick charge!*

The next chapter will address those who do not have any difficult stories or losses in their past but still struggle with their self-esteem and perhaps don't even know why.

Learn it, live it, and inspire others! *Quick Charge Your Life! Unshakable Self-Esteem*

We must embrace pain and burn it as fuel for our journey.
– **Kenji Miyazawa**

One thing I ask from the Lord, this only do I seek: that I may dwell in the house of the Lord all the days of my life, to gaze on the beauty of the Lord and to seek him in his temple.
— Psalm 27:4 (NIV)

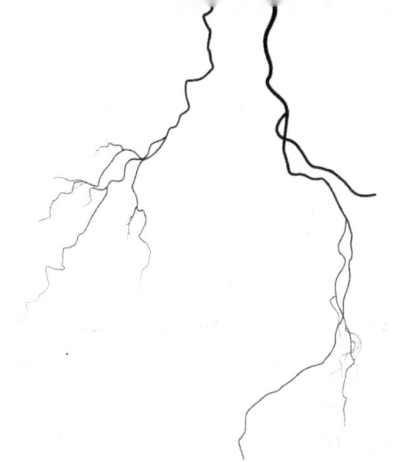

CHAPTER FOURTEEN

The Mirror Is Your Friend

One of the more common reasons many people struggle with their self-esteem and/or self-image is because of the image they see from head to toe when they gaze into a mirror. This struggle is especially true for women, but many men are also affected by a lack of healthy self-esteem.

When you look into a mirror, you form an opinion and grade what you think you see and know about yourself. However, your brain processes either positive or negative information back to your mind that might well not be really accurate information. If you like what you see, then your brain relays good or passing grades that bring joy, pride, pleasure, satisfaction, comfort, discipline, success, and many other positive signals. However, if your brain receives signals from the eye sensors that reject the image it sees, then bad or failing grades such as doubt, disappointment, failure, sadness, fear, hate, despair, frustration, and many other negative signals are relayed to the mind.

If you give yourself a failing grade, you might begin a dialogue like the following with yourself. "How did I get so heavy or fat?" "Why am I all skin and bones?" Why do I have so many wrinkles?" Why can't I be prettier or better looking?" "What's with the gray hair all of a sudden?" "Why do I look so old or so young or so____?" You continue to bombard yourself with an endless list of self-sabotaging questions.

Yet the issue goes even deeper. You see, humans try to determine if what they're doing is good or bad. Your reflection is staring back at you as you try to answer life questions as well. You begin to grade who you are as a person and whether or not you're doing enough to be acceptable. If you determine that you are doing fairly well in life or at least good enough, then you give yourself a passing grade. However, if on the other hand, you determine that the image staring back at you is not doing well, then you give yourself a failing grade.

If you give yourself a failing grade, you may start to question whether or not the signals being transmitted back to your brain are really worth the effort and pain to make whatever changes you might feel need to be made both externally and or internally.

Do you want to know a secret? The mirror really does **not** know whether that frame or shape is too skinny, too fat, too old, too this or too that. The mirror does not know if you're doing well in life or poorly. It only knows how to reflect or mirror the image that is placed in front of it. The mirror cannot differentiate shapes, sizes, age, race, religion, intelligence, life performance, etc. when you gaze into it! The mirror does not tell you that you are too skinny, too fat, too tall, too short, too poor, too dumb, too good or too ____.

So, what if for a moment you could be the mirror and not grade yourself as "good" or "bad" when you look into it? You do not grade or draw any conclusions other than you know it is you. You don't criticize or praise; you offer no judgmental opinions at all. I'll let you ponder that question for now.

The Mirror Is Your Friend

Obviously, mirrors are certainly useful when you are shaving, putting on makeup, brushing your hair, putting on clothes, brushing your teeth or any number of tasks as you groom and prep. But why do humans look into that mirror and try to asses or grade what it is they see looking back at them? I have even heard some say it's a way of connecting with yourself so you know you are really here. I feel one of the primary reasons we look into the mirror is for answers as to how we're doing, but I believe that reasoning is flawed.

Do you realize that what YOU see when you look at the reflection of your image coming back at you is NOT what OTHERS see when they look at you? You might think you look better in that mirror than how others see you! But if you have a low self-esteem, more often than not I believe that others look at you much more favorably than you see yourself.

Let me ask you again: why can't you just be the mirror? Why can't you just use the mirror to reflect your image without forming any judgment or grade for what you see?

The answer to that question is you have already formed your opinion—long before you even looked into the mirror. Yet you still look into the mirror, hoping it will tell you a different story. I see only one problem with that hope. The mirror does not know how to tell a story or make any judgments or form an opinion. The mirror can only reflect back whatever image is placed in front of it, period.

The other reason you look into the mirror is to see if the grade you might have given yourself on a prior occasion has improved or become worse. If you have a low self-esteem, then you are always searching for even the slightest grade improvement that you might be able to give yourself.

Allow me to bring these thoughts into a proper perspective and to help you see exactly how flawed your image and life assessment grading system is. As I continue to stress the importance of living the *quick-charge life,* I strongly encourage you to seek the Lord first and develop a positive image mindset based on the thoughts He has of you—instead of your own opinion and erroneous grading scale. What you need to understand is that your assessment of how well or how poorly you are doing is flawed. Your limited human perspective and the condition of your body with its mercurial variations distort your evaluations.

God does not form an opinion of what He sees based on the frame or the accomplishments or lack of accomplishments in any person's life. All that He does is **LOVE** every person unconditionally regardless of that person's life performance, accomplishments, his bodily condition or internal makeup.

The truth is, no matter how hopeless and wayward you are or how successful and disciplined you are, it will not give you a higher or lower grade in God's eyes. Your life's work has no bearing on God's love for you! He does not love one person more than another. His love is the same for every single human in the world. His forgiveness, healing, grace, and mercy are freely available to anyone regardless of any passing or failing grades they may try to assess upon themselves.

So, when you look in the mirror, tell yourself that you are LOVED! Tell yourself that you are a beloved child of God. Tell yourself that the Lord will give you the strength to make the changes or improvements that you can make. Tell yourself that you are someone worth believing in.

For now, you do not have to feel it, and you do not even need to believe it yourself because the Lord has it handled. However, you do need to discipline yourself to tell yourself that God loves you over and over no matter what. I highly recommend that you say it out loud repeatedly when you look in the mirror so you can see yourself saying it. You can even say it silently inside. Tell yourself throughout the day that you are valuable and loved.

Next, remind yourself that others do not see you the same way you see yourself nor do they perceive you as you perceive yourself. You can change your image simply by living with a positive mindset and giving yourself the freedom to enjoy life more. Remember, that everyone deals with his own issues, so others are really not that concerned if you're overweight, too skinny, too old or too whatever. Also remember that there will always be people who are far worse off than you!

So, although you cannot be a mirror, you can do your best! When you look at yourself, do not pass judgments or form an opinion too quickly. Try to look at that image staring back at you and acknowledge it is you. Remind yourself that what you don't like about yourself that can be changed can be improved—if you really want to improve these areas. Keep in mind that the mirror is not telling you that you must make a change or demanding that you make any adjustments. The mirror has no hidden agenda or any opinion of you at all.

The mirror is your friend; it reflects without judgment, without shame, without praise, and without any opinions at all. So, enjoy the reflection in the mirror because it's your friend without any judgments, demands, opinions or concerns.

Some might still be thinking, *God may be love, but He does not know me. How can He love me?*

The fact is, He knows if you're disciplined or not with your diet. He knows your thoughts and whether or not you simply do not care enough to make any changes in your life. Yes, I can assure you that God does know you well. He knows your thoughts, hopes, dreams, hurts, and disappointments. **However**, no matter what you think of yourself or have done, God still **loves** you.

God is willing and able to help you make the changes you can, and He will give you comfort and understanding for the things you don't understand or can't change. He loves you for who you are, and He knows **exactly** what He created you to be. So, trust that He knows you better than you'll ever know yourself. Perhaps you will decide today to speak words of encouragement and allow those self-professed positive words to inspire you to move past your perceived limitations and boldly step into the life you were born to create.

Psalm 139:1-6 (NCV), God Knows Everything

For the director of music. A psalm of David.

> *Lord, you have examined me and know all about me. ²You know when I sit down and when I get up. You know my thoughts before I think them. ³You know where I go and where I lie down. You know everything I do. ⁴Lord, even before I say a word, you already know it. ⁵You are all around me—in front and in back—and have put your hand on me. ⁶Your knowledge is amazing to me; it is more than I can understand.*

Learn it, live it, and inspire others! *Quick Charge Your Life! Unshakable Self-Esteem*

A good man brings good things out of the good stored up in him, and an evil man brings evil things out of the evil stored up in him.
— Matthew 12:35 (NIV)

The Mirror Is Your Friend

If you hear a voice within you say "you cannot paint," then by all means paint, and that voice will be silenced.

–Vincent van Gogh

To be yourself in a world that is constantly trying to make you something else is the greatest accomplishment.

– Ralph Waldo Emerson

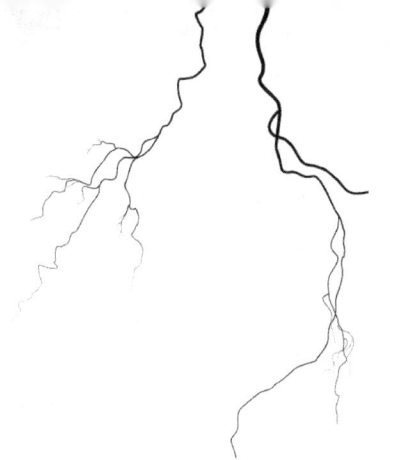

CHAPTER FIFTEEN

Addictions

I am so thankful for my many friends and family members who have overcome drug and/or alcohol addiction. They must wake up and fight a battle within themselves every single day of their lives to stay clean and sober. I cannot identify personally with this particular addictive lifestyle, but I know many people whom I love dearly who are now clean. Some must fight the demons daily that want to pull them back into the life they so desperately want to avoid.

A few years ago when I worked at a church, I tried to minister to a certain young man who had a drinking problem. Sadly, he would continually relapse and go back to drinking although he would openly confess that it was not a life he wanted to live. I watched him seemingly find himself time and time again, but usually within a few months, he would eventually return to his drunken ways.

One evening at church when he had been sober for nearly a month, I asked him, "Why do you think you always go back to drinking?"

He answered, "I guess it is because it's much easier to just go back to the life I know rather than face a life unknown."

I decided to dig a little deeper and asked, "What scares you about the life unknown when it could be a life filled with so much promise and hope?"

"Well, because I have no idea what promise and hope look like from my perspective. When I drink, at least I know what to expect, and I have learned to survive in this world. It never disappoints me."

What he really meant was that it always disappointed him, but that paradigm was familiar to him, so he learned to accept it as being all he would ever know.

People cannot seem to break away from many other addictions as well. When they give into that addiction, they feel guilt and shame, and often promise themselves they will never go there again. During my days of church ministry, I met with others as well who struggled with various addictions. The conversations were often the same. Most people would tell me that it was the last time they would ever fall prey to what enslaved them. They would boldly proclaim that they had finally learned their lesson and knew this time they were going to beat whatever addiction they were fighting. However, we would usually end up having the same conversation a few months later.

So, what do you do if you are one who is reading this chapter right now, and you know you have a low self-esteem because of an addiction you simply cannot beat? Of course, I'm not referring to only drugs or alcohol.

Here are the answers I can offer for your situation. First, if you have not already sought help, I would encourage you to do some research and find someone who can connect you to

Addictions

the proper support group or to people who are trained to give you help and support in the area of addiction you need help.

I would also tell you to ask God to heal whatever thoughts you have that lead you to relapse and ask Him to instill hope. I would implore you to realize you have the strength within you to see your mountain, and you can choose to climb it every day. Every time you feel the urge to relapse, bite into the lemon (of addiction), and then take a step up your mountain instead. Every step is a victory! Yes, it's a hard climb at times, but the views as you rise above your situation and see wonderful successes as you climb higher up the mountain are worth it!

Whenever you feel the urge to relapse, you need to remember to *quick charge*! If a difficult situation arises and you feel tempted, then bite into the lemon and break the pattern with a positive image or thought. Seek the Lord first as soon as you awaken each day and continue throughout the day until you go to sleep at night.

Remember the mirror illustration in the previous chapter? Look into the mirror and realize that the mirror does not know your struggles. The mirror will not pass judgment on you. The mirror cannot know your past or your future. The mirror neither believes in you nor doubts you. The mirror simply reflects an image. Everyone around you, including yourself, will have some sort of opinion, expectation, and belief or conclusion as to your outcome—good or bad. However, the mirror has no judgment or expectations at all. So, look into that mirror and see a clear slate that can be filled with positive affirmations and hope.

I could tell you that I believe you can overcome anything, and I do believe you can create a strong, positive self-image of yourself if you will implement the tools in this book to help you overcome, but I am only human with my own faults and shortcomings. The tools I present are valuable and will help you to overcome anything in your life—if you choose to be open and use the methods presented.

However, the One who created you is your best source for overcoming anything you face. I believe with all my heart that if you will seek the Lord first and apply the *quick-charge* concepts and seek the support of wise people, you will climb your mountain to victory!

I want you to see a vision! As you climb your mountain, you will face fewer and fewer temptations. The allurement of temptations will still come, but as you trust in the Lord and keep climbing, they become less and less tempting. The farther up the mountain you climb in life, the cleaner the air, the better the view, and the sweeter the victory. You need not climb to the top of the mountain to experience the victory. You can begin to see the victory when you start to climb, and that, my friend, will build an unshakable self-esteem.

No temptation has overtaken you except what is common to mankind. And God is faithful; he will not let you be tempted beyond what you can bear. But when you are tempted, he will also provide a way out so that you can endure it.
— 1 Corinthians 10:13 (NIV)

I often hear people say that God will not give you more than you can handle. However, if you read the Scripture, it does not say you will not be given more than you can handle. The verse says He will not let you be tempted beyond what you can bear.

You may still be faced with many difficult situations in life. The Lord does not always take away those situations,

Addictions

but what He does do is not allow you to be tempted beyond what you can bear. The heaviness of life can block you if you choose not to move things aside and continue to see yourself climbing your mountain. It can literally be more than you can bear at times, but that is not a reason to give in and relapse. Your difficulties will not be more temptation than you can handle; rather, it is simply more weight than you can bear. Yes, at times life might feel like it is more than you can handle, but GOD can handle those times for you. I hope you will realize the weight is not yours to handle! You can choose to turn it over to the Lord. He already handled your weight when He died on the cross. Give all your burdens to Him and choose to climb above the difficulties.

> *Humble yourselves, therefore, under God's mighty hand, that he may lift you up in due time.* [7]*Cast all your anxiety on him because he cares for you.*
> — 1 PETER 5:6-7 (NIV)

Learn it, live it, and inspire others! *Quick Charge Your Life! Unshakable Self-Esteem*

> *Never lose hope. Storms make people stronger and never last forever.*
> — ROY T. BENNETT

> *It always seems impossible until it's done.*
> — NELSON MANDELA

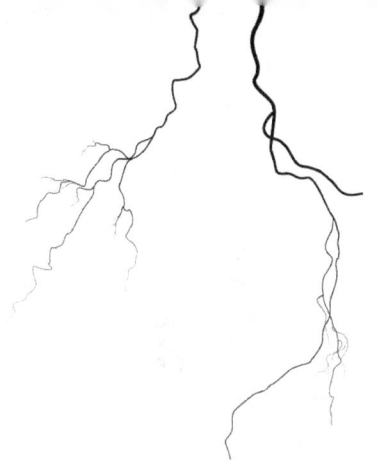

CHAPTER SIXTEEN

What About Me?

Perhaps you read the stories about people who were born without limbs or had birth defects that left them with bad deformities, but you really cannot relate. Maybe you were never subjected to any kind of violent abuse that would point to why you feel so lost. Perhaps you find yourself still searching for answers to the reasons why you feel the way you do, but thus far, you still have no definitive reasons as to why. Nothing you seek or try seems to give you any direction or answers. What do you do when you have never really experienced anything life-altering enough to clearly contribute to your low self-esteem? To make it even more confusing, you have the Lord in your life and you have tried to live a good life, but you still find yourself searching for answers as to why you cannot see a positive self-image of yourself.

The fact is you may not be able to find any definitive catalyst in your life that would clearly explain why you feel the way you do about yourself. My friend, that's okay! Life is a journey, and you, like anyone else, can climb your mountain to victory. If such is the case, how do you figure out how to believe in yourself enough to break out of the life you have and into the life God designed for you?

Well, the first step you take is to ask! Yes, simply ask the Lord and see what He has to say. Taking that step sounds simple, but have you spent time reading the Word and talking to God about the way you feel? Begin with asking Him for guidance and wisdom.

The next step is listening for His answers—though not in an audible way. What do you sense He is saying when you pray about your dreams and goals?

The next step is a question to ask yourself. If you believed in yourself and liked who you were then, what would you do? Let's just assume for a moment that tomorrow morning you awakened with an unshakable self-esteem. Now, with that new frame of mind, what do you really want out of life? Do you have dreams churning inside of you? If you could only find the courage, what dream or goal would you currently be pursuing?

Once you have some dreams and goals in your mind, write them down! I realize believing that the dreams inside of you will really come true can be difficult. Dreaming can be especially challenging if you have previously given in to the negative self-images in your mind. When you've lost hope, you can feel like your dreams are not within reach, but you must look past those thoughts. Establishing your goals and dreams is one of the keys to moving forward.

The next step you should take is start a journal. Disciplining yourself to keep a journal can be powerful! When you journal, you need to record your daily thoughts. Then weave positive affirmations into your notes, using the techniques I shared in the chapter on journaling.

The next step to take is to start feeding your mind with positive thoughts from the moment you awaken until the time

What About Me?

you go to sleep at night. Following through on this step takes work in the beginning and will always require discipline, but being doubtful and negative takes as much work as it does to be positive, so you might as well choose to be positive!

Tell yourself the following affirmations: "I am proud of you for making strides to create change." "You are going to be a success!" "It's okay to like me!" "I will climb to the top of my mountain."

I know, I may sound like a broken record as I have covered these techniques and concepts in various ways throughout the book. The reason I put so much emphasis on it is because I KNOW these concepts work. I've applied them to my own life, but more than that, the *quick-charge* method has worked for thousands of people!

> *The first time you say something, it's heard; the second time, it's recognized; the third time, it's learned.*
> — JOHN MAXWELL

I am not implying or even suggesting that praying, thinking positive, and journaling will suddenly give you a perfect life or make everything clear. Perfect lives do not exist! But I can tell you that living life this way has given me an extraordinary life, and thus, the *quick-charge life* has built my unshakable self-esteem.

You will never have a perfect life in this world, and you will need to work hard at times to keep climbing your mountain, but you can hold your head high, knowing you are making strides to better yourself every day. I am confident that if you will discipline yourself to be consistent, you will build unshakable self-esteem. Don't worry if you do not have all the answers or be concerned if you cannot understand why you struggle with your self-esteem. If you start climbing your mountain, it's only a matter of time until you will begin to see better views!

Learn it, live it, and inspire others! *Quick Charge Your Life! Unshakable Self-Esteem*

There are two answers to every question—God's answer and everybody else's—and everybody else is wrong when they disagree with him.

— Tony Evans

Trust in the Lord with all your heart and lean not on your own understanding; ⁶in all your ways submit to him, and he will make your paths straight.

— Proverbs 3:5-6 (NIV)

Conclusion

I may not know you personally, and we may never meet face to face here on earth, but for what it is worth, my friend, I do believe in you. I can honestly say with all the passion inside of me that I know you have the power within you to rise above your circumstances and build an unshakable self-esteem. The battle that is waged between your ears can be greater than anything you ever face. People can create incredible value out of their life when they simply change their mind and choose to see themselves as victors rather than victims.

If you look around, you will find people every day with incredible physical challenges who go on to create lives of great value and inspire millions to do the same. You will find people who overcame addictions and built awe-inspiring lives. You can find people who simply could not figure out who they were or why they had such a poor image of themselves. Thankfully, they finally found the strength within to climb their mountain and reach great new heights in their life.

I know that taking a step up the mountain instead of a step down can be difficult at times. Believing you will ever be one of those who can achieve your wildest dreams and see yourself as worthy can also be a challenge. Perhaps you have no desire to change the world; you simply want to like yourself. Regardless of your mindset for whatever it is you want to achieve in life, I know at the end of the day all anyone really wants is to simply like themselves.

What is wonderful about an unshakable self-esteem is you can create that in your mind! When you change your mind, then you can find the strength and courage to make the modifications in your life that can be transformed. You will find roadblocks at times and lemons will come your way. You can develop the mindset to bite into those lemons and claim victory over any adversity life throws your way.

I will conclude this book with a powerful thought I heard while doing my daily research and study. I was watching an online video of Jim Rohn as he was inspiring a room full of people. As usual, he shared an illustration that ignited a powerful *quick-charge* in me that I want to pass on to you as well.

He asked the audience a simple question: **how long does a mother wait to see her baby walk?** Does she reach a certain point and say, "Well, I guess it will never happen, so let's just forget about it"?

Of course not! She waits **UNTIL** the baby walks! She will continue to encourage the baby **UNTIL**.... She believes her baby can walk **UNTIL**.... She simply encourages and waits **UNTIL** it happens.

You can achieve anything you set your mind to. You can climb your mountain! So, how long will you wait to see your life in a new and powerful way?

UNTIL!

Conclusion

You can use everything that comes your way—good or bad—and use it to climb your mountain and rise above **UNTIL** you achieve unshakable self-esteem!

The great news is, when it happens, it happens—just like the baby suddenly learns to walk for the first time! Stay with it **UNTIL** it happens!

Learn it, live it, and inspire others! *Quick Charge Your Life! Unshakable Self-Esteem*

What lies behind you and what lies in front of you, pales in comparison to what lies inside of you.
— RALPH WALDO EMERSON

You must do the things you think you cannot do.
— ELEANOR ROOSEVELT

"Therefore encourage one another and build each other up, just as in fact you are doing."
— 1 THESSALONIANS 5:11 (NIV)

Books

Tommy Turner's first book simply titled *Quick Charge Your Life* is available on Amazon and Barnes & Noble.

Tuning pianos for many amazing musicians and entertainers over the years including Johnny Cash, June Carter, Ronnie Milsap, Lyle Lovett, and JoAnn Castle of "Lawrence Welk" fame, have led to incredible quick-charge moments in Tommy Turner's life. In his first book, *Quick Charge Your Life*, Tommy shares an inspiring encounter with legendary singers, Johnny Cash and his wife June, that forever shaped his life. Discover how *your* daily encounters can forever quick charge your life and the lives of those with whom you cross paths...

Coming Soon:

Tommy's Third Book in the Quick Charge series!

Quick Charge Your Life:

Crush Panic Attacks and Calm Anxiety

Contact

For more information about the *quick-charge concept*, please visit us on the web at http://quickchargeyourlife.com

To learn more about the author, Tommy Turner visit http://tommyturner.com

CPSIA information can be obtained
at www.ICGtesting.com
Printed in the USA
LVHW081822200920
666593LV00025B/666